The Essence of
Donald J. Trump
☆
Lessons on Achieving Success

The
Essence of
Donald J. Trump

Lessons on Achieving Success

Laurie Luongo, SPHR

Former VP of the
Trump Hotel Collection

CKBooks

Contact Laurie Luongo at LaurieLuongo.com
Publisher's Cataloging-In-Publication Data

Names: Luongo, Laurie, author.
Title: The essence of Donald J. Trump : lessons on achieving success / Laurie Luongo, SPHR, former VP of the Trump Hotel Collection.
Description: New Glarus, WI : CKBooks Publishing, [2019]
Identifiers: ISBN 9781949085105
Subjects: LCSH: Trump, Donald L. (Donald Lynn), 1945- | Trump Organization (New York, N.Y.) | Presidents--United States--Biography. | Businesspeople--United States--Biography. | Successful people--United States--Biography. | LCGFT: Biographies.
Classification: LCC E913 .L86 2019 | DDC 973.933092--dc23

LCCN: 2019907447

Cover image ~ White House photo/Alamy stock photo

CKBooks Publishing
PO Box 214
New Glarus, WI
53574
ckbookspublishing.com

Dedication

I dedicate this book to my beloved mother, Mary Cava Robito Luongo. I am the second of Mom's eleven children and she was my best friend. Mom never learned to drive, yet she got everywhere and traveled the world. She did not graduate from high school, yet was smarter than some who hold advanced degrees. My mom taught me everything I know about hospitality and how to treat people. She was loved by people all over the globe. She was and always will be my inspiration to lead a life of purpose, kindness, and compassion.

Table of Contents

Foreword

The American Dream is a phrase that's been used for decades. My grandparents came to America from Italy in search of it. My parents talked about it in the context of people like them who wanted a good education for their children. My generation, the baby boomers, robustly went after their dreams with gusto. Now in retirement, those who are deemed successful have the financial security to enjoy their golden years. Success comes in all shapes and sizes, and in every walk of life. Some equate success with wealth, power, position and status. In whatever way it looks or is described it is something that people go after, often, their entire lives. After spending more than three decades in corporate America, I decided to write about how people have found success, some in unlikely ways. I researched individuals in order to read their life journey and what they did and did not do to gain success. All of the people I discuss in this book utilized many of the same techniques and traits I discuss. Some of the people will not be known to the reader, yet they are famous (or infamous) in their field. Others had very challenging and interesting paths, while some used their talents and gifts to do something extraordinary.

This book, in addition to capturing the traits that Donald Trump employed to become the 45th president, gives the reader examples of strategies that others have used to gain success. Each chapter focuses on one trait and how it has been used to reap rewards either in business or life. It is a discovery which should give hope to students and those starting their careers that anything is possible. For people in leadership positions, it's a deeper dive into how to use the traits to their advantage. For those who are out of the workforce, it is an opportunity to view behaviors that can result in a more purposeful life. Each chapter tells stories of how certain individuals parlayed a specific trait or behavior to reach their goals. The reader will take away simple strategies for everyday life to make it more meaningful and, in business, more rewarding.

It is often said that timing is everything. After almost three decades of experience in hospitality, I rolled the dice and took advantage of a once-in-a-lifetime chance to start a new brand of hotels. Along the way, almost five years from start to finish, I learned of the pillars of success that helped Donald J. Trump become our 45th President. I had an insider's view of the Trump Organization, and got to know the Trump "kids" (as we affectionately referred to them). Together, we started a luxury hotel collection under the tutelage of Donald J. Trump. It was the most incredible job of my career – not because of Mr. Trump, but because I took a risk and participated in starting a new brand from the ground up. Challenges can be hugely rewarding or downright failures. I was not promised success but I jumped in with both feet. It was a vast undertaking that took much time, effort, and determination. The journey was fast, exciting, and one I will always remember. I invite you to read these stories of success and how you, too, can reach for the stars.

Chapter One

Passion – Your Purpose in Life
Focus on Your Goals

If you can tell stories, create characters, devise incidents, and have sincerity and passion, it doesn't matter a damn how you write

~ Somerset Maugham

For the first time in their history, the Academy Awards was without a formal host in 2019. While unconventional, the show did go on and it included the usual political statements. Some comments were more profound and have people still talking. Lady Gaga (Stefani Germanotta), "reminded us all how to truly succeed – by working (smartly toward your goals, and following your passion."[1] Gaga told the packed house, earlier mesmerized by her and Bradley Cooper's singing performance of the winning song, "Shallow," "If you have a dream fight for it ... there's a discipline for passion. And it's not about how many times you get rejected, or you fall down, or you're beaten up. It's about how many times you stand up, and are brave, and you keep going."[2]

These words could have been spoken by my former boss, Donald J. Trump, when he was a businessman, a candidate for the Republican Party nomination, and now as president. This chapter will discuss many facets of Mr. Trump's passion, his first pillar of success. I will also tell powerful stories of others who, with passion, made their dreams come true or helped to change the world for the better.

Many companies use the word passion – in mission statements, employee orientation, staff development, and in meetings. Advertising and marketing firms often invoke passion or what they see as passionate people in television and print ads. Mike Lindell, creator of "MyPillow," begins his television ads with "As you know, my passion is to help each and every one of you get the best sleep of your life." Before inventing "MyPillow" in 2004, Mike operated numerous small businesses in his home state of Minnesota. One of his ventures was a tavern, and during that time he became associated with people who dealt drugs. In his early twenties he became addicted to cocaine and alcohol and subsequently lost his home, his wife of 20 years, and nearly his "MyPillow" business as well. But Mike was determined and passionate to become sober and with much effort and assistance, he did so in 2009. According to Bloomberg: "He had no credit and wanted $1 million in goods. Lindell was so passionate that we decided to give him a shot."[3]. He is also proud and passionate to say on television, in meetings and roundtables, that he produces all of his products in the United States. His business grew rapidly and he now has a second factory and sales of $250 million.[4] His television ads, featuring him as the spokesperson, have aired more than 2.5 million times in 15 years.[5] Mike has added other products to his company: a pillow topper, a doggie bed and, Giza sheets generating even more jobs and revenue.

Here is a guy who was on the path to destruction, but who was passionate about sleep and pillows and is now a millionaire. Mike produced a documentary in 2017, *The Mike Lindell Story: An American Dream* about overcoming addiction and building his multimillion-dollar company. Mike is also passionate about helping those who are addicts. He created the Lindell Foundation, which began solely to assist "MyPillow" employees who were addicts. After a special project for Hurricane Harvey survivors which included donating thousands of pillows, the foundation stretched its reach to help veterans, active duty military, and those with cancer. Mike's Lindell Recovery Network was highlighted in an Opioid Crisis meeting at the White House on October 24, 2018. Since then, Mike has given $1million to an independent production of a pro-life film, *Unplanned,* which is slated for the big screen. He was one of many speakers at the 2019 annual Conservative Political Action Conference (CPAC) in which he stated his belief that President Trump was "chosen by God" to run for the White House.[6] Mike was on the streets ten years ago and now he's visiting the Oval Office. His passion, grit, and determination took him on a different and better path and he has "arrived." While many may disagree with his political views, you cannot help but admire this man who with great passion and resolve overcame addiction and has turned his life around. "About politics, Mike Lindell is unapologetic. About pillows, he's passionate."[7]

What is it about passion that strikes a chord with people and makes it a highly desirable trait?

Passion resonates in every arena – for example, sports fans are often referred to as passionate about their teams. I am a passionate Red Sox fan. Whether they are in first place or last in their division, my passion is evident when I speak about my team and Red Sox Nation. During baseball season, starting with spring training, I follow the Sox. Years ago, people would often ask me if I bet on the team. I do not bet – I am just a passionate and devoted fan. The passion for my team began with my dad, who took us to Fenway Park when we were kids, and it has become part of the Luongo DNA as we have passed that passion on to my nephew and his two sons. When I lived in Kansas City, which is a great baseball town, I cheered for the Royals unless they were playing the Sox. My brother, who was born on the same day as Ted Williams, was my roommate. He worked nights, so I was asleep when he arrived home from work. Each morning, regardless of the standings or how early or late in the season, he left a note on the dining room table with just two words, either "we won" or "we lost." To this day, for me, he is the greatest Sox fan ever and his devotion never wanes. It can, however, be brutal to be around him when watching a Red Sox game, particularly this year as the team has gotten off to a rather bad start.

In business, when hiring new people, passion is something that interviewers look for in the way a candidate speaks about their previous jobs and what they do for a living. In their personal lives, some people champion a cause about which they are passionate. Maria Shriver, the Kennedy cousin, has devoted much time and energy to the Women's Alzheimer's Movement. Maria, who previously worked in the news business and on TV, was also first lady of California. She has enough wealth to sit back and do nothing or travel the world, yet she actively volunteers and advocates for numerous causes. When you read her blogs and website or listen to her speak about Alzheimer's, you hear the passion in her voice – a passion to learn everything we can about this disease and to find a cure in our lifetime. Maria's dad died from Alzheimer's, as my mom did. It is often the case that people volunteer or chose causes to align with when they or a family member has been impacted. I believe that instills in them a will to do something about the particular cause they are championing. And Maria is a consummate professional who is passionate about that cause. Maria, I am confident, learned about passion for others through her parents and the legacy that each of them left her to serve others. In a recent *Sunday Paper*, she talked about a conversation with Chelsea Handler in which she was asked "What are the two areas you want to be great in?" Maria says, "It was the author's message that if we want to rise from 'good to great' in our work and in our lives, then we must identify what we're most passionate about and apply the bulk of our effort and energy there...."[8]

Maria's dad, Sargent Shriver, was named the program's first director of the Peace Corps[9] under President Kennedy. The Peace Corps resulted from JFK's dedication to public service and his belief that Americans should serve their country and the world. It became an official program run by the government, established by executive order on March 1, 1961. During a speech to 10,000 students at the University of Michigan in October 1960, the future president asked the students "How many...would be willing to serve their country and the cause of peace by living and working in the developing world?"[10] Since its inception over 50 years ago, there have been more than 200,000 volunteers who serve in 141 countries around the world. Maria's mom, Eunice Kennedy Shriver, started the Special Olympics,[11] which after her death has been continued by her son. These are passionate people who believe in the cause they give so much time, money, and energy to promoting. Eunice Kennedy Shriver is referred to again in my chapter, "Think Big."

When I was hired by the Trump Organization, I learned of Mr. Trump's "pillars of success," which are passion, drive, and enthusiasm. Early on, I came to understand how he and his family used those traits to become successful business entrepreneurs. It does not imply that every project or venture they embarked upon was a success. In fact, since I left the Trump Organization, three of the hotels I helped open are no longer affiliated with the Trump brand. Interestingly enough, most successful people, in whatever their occupation, tell stories of failure. Often it is their persistence and drive that keep them going and allow them to attain their goals and definition of success.

Passion is the first of Mr. Trump's "pillars of success." It's interesting to me that he uses the word pillar. People do seem to use the language of the business in which they work. It's no coincidence that companies seek passionate individuals to work for them. Passionate people in any endeavor are typically more energetic, productive, and positive. Mr. Trump sought the most positive and passionate people to work in his hotels with the belief that, if an individual possessed certain characteristics like passion, the technical part of the specific job could be taught. Let's face it, hospitality is not rocket science. If someone is passionate, you can teach him or her to perform a task. You can also have the best taskmaster there is, but, without passion that person can negatively impact your business.

Whatever Trump does, he does it with passion. As a businessman, Donald J. Trump was passionate about his buildings, his company, and the vast holdings he created. Mr. Trump's passion fuels his energy, and that translates into setting specific goals. One of his goals was to create a hotel company. He partnered in Las Vegas with the owner of the now demolished Frontier Hotel to build the tallest structure in Las Vegas. They each owned 50 percent of the venture, and both have a penthouse suite in the hotel tower. There was enough land on the site for a second tower, which in the original plan was to open in 2009. Construction on the second tower never began – the idea was put on hold and eventually scrapped when the economy took a downturn in 2007 – but even that did not stop Trump from forging ahead.

Mr. Trump was well known for making good deals for himself with partners and vendors. By doing so he trimmed his costs and was able to challenge all involved to come in under budget and complete the project on time or ahead of schedule. In Las Vegas we were able to do both. In his first presidential debate, on October 12, 2016, candidate Trump casually mentioned, when speaking about making America more prosperous, that his Washington, D.C. hotel was ahead of schedule and under budget. He takes great pride in being able to boast about such accomplishments. There were approximately 84 million people tuned in. His crowd of supporters looked inspired and motivated, and candidate Trump's confidence and passion were on display. Leaders have great influence over people, and sometimes do not fully understand how what they say translates into behavior. At the time, the executives working in Las Vegas were simply doing their jobs, and we were passionate about the product we represented, which gave us added impetus to reach the goals set for the enterprise. It also made going to work each day and working long hours and weeks much more fun. Mr. Trump has said, "You cannot be successful without passion. If you don't love what you're doing, if you don't have passion for it – forget it."

As the vice president of human resources, I was acutely aware that our employees needed to be passionate about their jobs. Our leaders had worked with people in the past who we wanted on our team, because each of them was passionate about guest service. We had also worked in hotels with others who had decades of experience; however, they did not possess the passion about their work that we required. Early on, each executive went through training to learn about Mr. Trump's three pillars of success, and passion was key. If we interviewed someone who had the skill set but lacked passion/ energy, we passed on that individual. We were fortunate at the time that there was no lack of qualified people in Las Vegas, and a plethora of folks who salivated at the chance to work for a Trump property. The managers who interviewed the candidates were passionate in how they explained the property, what the job entailed, and what we envisioned as success (i.e., unparalleled service).

In fact, another thing about Mr. Trump's passion is the concept he came up with many years ago, before folks had data bases and tracked guests' personal preferences. I was told we would have an "Attache" department, and I had to ask for more information on what the department was responsible for, what the employees would do, and so on. The Attache Department is a step up from the traditional butler and concierge services offered in many hotels. A Trump Attache carefully notes every guest preference and keeps a detailed history so that in future stays at a Trump Collection Hotel the guest is made to feel like it's a return home. The Trump Attache also arranges everything from in-room chefs to private jets. On the current Trump Hotels website, under "At Your Service," it says that the Trump Attache delivers personalized attention without intrusion, where desires are intuited and requests are anticipated. I had the opportunity early on in my Trump career to experience the Trump Attache firsthand. I was going to Trump Tower for meetings and staying at Trump International on Columbus Circle. After making a reservation, I received a call from an employee identifying herself as a Trump Attache. She proceeded to ask several questions, including what my favorite water was, if I drank coffee and, if so, how I liked it, my newspaper of choice, and anything else I may have wanted upon arrival. I was curious to see the result when I went to the hotel as a guest.

When I checked into my room, the newspaper I had requested was there along with the water I asked for and half and half for my coffee. In addition, on the desk was a note from the general manager with a packet of personalized stationery, envelopes, and business cards, as well as an ornate basket filled with fruit. I was now really sold on Trump Hotels as a guest and as an employee. The Attache tradition is still going strong today. In fact, I recently read on the Trump Hotels website that "Guests of all 13 Trump hotels can expect personalized service thanks to the brand's signature programs. Trump Attache services include personal shopping and pre-arrival grocery delivery." The Attache concept was brilliant because, in addition to providing unparalleled service, the hotel was subtly inviting guests back.

One of my passions is customer service. Over my years in the hospitality industry I was amazed by the laissez-faire attitude displayed by many employees about service. I would remind people that the customer was paying our salaries. Some of the training we developed included such rudimentary things as not saying "I don't know" to a guest *and* expecting the guest to be fine with the employee not knowing an answer. I may not know a lot of things; however, I do know this: when a guest asks a question and an employee does not know the answer, it's our job to find out. And if that means we need some time to get the answer, it's also our job to follow up with the guest. Little things like that can set a company apart, especially today when the majority of companies have automated prompts answering phones and customers need to go through hoops simply to speak with someone. When we were teaching "telephone etiquette" as a seminar to all associates, it was not acceptable to place phones on voice mail. If I or anyone else was away from the desk, the phone had to be forwarded to a living, breathing person. This sounds like a basic tenet of customer service, yet it is not very common in today's business environment. The companies that are passionate about service and setting themselves apart are the ones that answer the phones.

One of our goals at Trump Hotel Collection was to provide unparalleled service. To accomplish that we had to train team members in each and every aspect of encounters with guests and how to effectively handle them to meet or exceed their expectations. We were passionate about the ability of an employee to anticipate a guest's needs. For example, if a guest approached the front desk to check in with a small child and the pre-assigned room did not have a crib, the employee would immediately ask the guest if a crib was needed. This meant the guest did not have to go into the room, see that there was no crib, and then call the front desk to request one.

I first met Mr. Trump at the "topping off" ceremony at Trump International Las Vegas, which occurred on a beautiful spring day, May 25, 2007. The topping off ceremony officially acknowledges that the building exterior is completed. A handful of us were on site at approximately 6:00 a.m. We ensured that the staging area was pristine, that we had our places set, that the gifts for all guests were properly displayed, the "greeters" were positioned perfectly, and everything down to the smallest detail was taken care of. The topping off ceremonies in Las Vegas are typically newsworthy, and this one *was* news! Mr. Trump, accompanied by his bodyguard Keith Schiller, arrived in a limousine and all of us, including the media, the mayor, and other dignitaries were eagerly waiting for the boss to appear. The construction crew was there, as it is always appropriate to thank them during the event. Mr. Trump was introduced by Stefanie Schaeffer, who was the winner of season six of *The Apprentice*. Until I began working for Trump, I had never watched *The Apprentice*. My mom was visiting me at the time, and I told her we must watch *The Apprentice* because I now worked for Mr. Trump. We watched the show together for the first time on April 9, 2007. In that episode, the Las Vegas property was featured. Mom made remarks about Mr. Trump's stature, how commanding his presence was when he entered a room, and his obvious self-confidence. Even at almost 80 years old, Mom was astute and very intuitive. *The Apprentice* winner that year went on to work in our pre-opening office for a short time, and then later on a one-year assignment for another Trump project. Mr. Trump spoke for only a few minutes, thanking everyone and showing his pride in constructing the tallest building in Las Vegas. After he spoke, he came over to the executive team and our general manager introduced him to each one of us. He then got into the limousine and departed.

In the fall of 2007, with two new properties open in Chicago and Las Vegas, Mr. Trump held a news conference in New York and announced the Trump Hotel Collection brand to the world. The press release stated "Trump Hotel Collection is the newest brand and the highest level of luxury hospitality available under the Trump name."[12] It went on to say that "Donald J. Trump, chairman and president of the Trump Organization, refers to the Trump Hotel Collection as "A natural extension of our (Trump) brand in the luxury sector of the hotel industry." His remarks exemplified the passion he has for his work, his brand, and his company. Mr. Trump has said, "If you don't have passion, everything you do will ultimately fizzle out or, at best, be mediocre. Is that how you want to live your life?" He was asked in a CNBC interview in June 2012 about his brand, and his response was: "Building a brand is very interesting. You need time, you need quality, you need success.... I've seen so many people over the years that are very smart, but they don't have passion. They just don't have that feeling of passion ... having enthusiasm, having passion is very, very important for success ... you need that enthusiasm, you need that passion, that drive."

Employees were very excited to read accounts of the press conference and proud to say we worked for the Trump Hotel Collection, which was set to expand on a global scale. Back in Las Vegas, we were receiving samples of beds, linens, and bathroom amenities from all over the world. There were discussions with the Trump kids about the products, what we believed the guest would like, what the competition offered, and how we could set ourselves apart, with money not being an object. Don, Ivanka, and Eric were passionate about the quality of everything in the guest rooms – from the type of coffeemaker to the guest bathrobes. The choice for the bed linens consisted of the finest sheets from Italy and duvet covers that were simply exquisite. In fact, Ivanka was so intimately involved that she personally selected the employee uniforms! She tells employees about that in the orientation video, and mentions that she thinks they will like them. On phone calls from New York that I participated in, typically at 6:00 a.m. PST, it was made known that Mr. Trump was quite passionate about spending his money on the best products, from Bosch dishwashers to Sub-Zero appliances. But this is better left for the chapter on negotiating.

In a tweet on March 10, 2014 @realdonald trump said, "Have passion, drive and enthusiasm? You can check out the @Trump Collection Careers here." In an interview Trump said, "Hire for passion and commitment first."[13] Businessman Trump used every opportunity to remind people of his pillars to success, and passion was number one. On the campaign trail, candidate Trump's passion was displayed at his rallies. Never have I seen a candidate for any election more passionate about campaigning than this Republican nominee for president. In my opinion, his passion went to a new and higher level than during his days as a businessman. Mr. Trump's passion for what he was doing morphed into energy, and he never faltered. I believe that his passion and energy, which seemed to increase as the months of the campaign went on, helped him get elected. Trump's base was equally passionate about voting for him and ensuring victory. The atmosphere at the campaign rallies was electric. Whether one likes Trump or not, he had people fired up and his supporters were passionate about him and his agenda.

President Trump's passion is most evident when he is on camera speaking on a topic about which he is passionate. For me, it is his love for America and his quest to make us great again, everything from securing our borders to immigration reform to tax cuts and healthcare reform. In his acceptance speech at the Republican National Convention, Trump declared, "I only want to admit individuals into our country who will support our values and love our people. Anyone who endorses violence, hatred or oppression is not welcome in our country and never will be."

These are the types of things that appealed to so many American voters. Candidate Trump was confident, tough, and relentless. He was a maverick on the campaign trail and usually unscripted. His passion fueled the fire in millions of voters, and he took full advantage of it. The passion he showed was seen by millions as different from the seasoned politicians who offered the people the usual rhetoric and promises of being a change agent in order to get elected. Trump used his passion to drive the political narrative, and it in turn drove millions to the polls to vote for him. It will be interesting for those much younger than I to read about the 2016 campaign in decades to come. Of this I am certain: "Donald J. Trump almost single-handedly harnessed discontent among 'forgotten Americans' despite running a guerilla-style grass roots campaign...."[14] He was brilliant at harnessing the power of those whom he described as the "forgotten Americans," and he played to their discontent.

The bottom line in any endeavor is to uncover feelings of passion – striving for that all-important emotional connection with the people who matter. In order for employees to be passionate at work, they must believe in whatever service or product they are representing or selling. I am always amazed when I ask employees who work in (for example) a restaurant, what they can tell me about a particular dish, and they respond that they have never tasted it so they cannot comment. I'm much more comfortable ordering something when a server tells me how delicious it is and can describe it in detail because he or she has tasted it. Hotels are no different. When you give the employees the opportunity to experience the check-in procedure, and to stay in a room as a guest, he or she will be able to upsell a guest because they have experienced it. Before a Trump Hotel opened for business, employees in guest-facing positions and those responsible for selling the rooms had the opportunity to stay in the hotel as a guest. Those employees would then critique the experience and give us feedback that often included making changes to a procedure or fixing something in the room. Doing things like this is smart business and can also be used as an employee incentive or reward.

I've always been curious about what fuels passion in human beings. Sometimes you can meet a person for the first time and within minutes discover where their passion lies. Some people live a lifetime without passion. In the business world, experts say that workers who are passionate produce more and are more efficient. In life, a lot of passionate people volunteer, advocate, and/or sit on boards that represent their cause. So how does one develop and exhibit passion? Start with training classes and exercises discussing passion. As leaders, ask:

- What does passion mean to you?

- Why are people passionate? Why not?

- What are you passionate about? Why?

- When was the last time you showed passion? (Not everyone can answer or describe what they were passionate about or when their passion developed.)

- Give examples of people you believe are passionate. What are they passionate about? How does that passion come through?

After a training session like the one described above we documented the information garnered, and that became the basis for the next session, which was about the concept of drive. After all of the sessions were completed, we introduced the core values which became the template for the company. In the new employee orientation, a core values card was given to every associate to carry in their pocket. Each property customized the "card" to include information specific to that hotel. The Trump card is not unlike that used by other hotel companies like the Ritz Carlton, for example. Their credo, which every associate is expected to recite at the drop of a hat, is "Ladies and Gentlemen taking care of Ladies and Gentlemen." Pre-eminent corporations teach and inspire employees to live out the culture and values of their company. It is an essential element of taking care of the guests, and of one another. Our vision statement was: to create the preeminent luxury hotel brand in the world. In order to do this, employees must possess the traits I am discussing in this book.

Whenever anyone in a leadership position asks me for advice on teaching their employees how to deal with guests, including following up and getting answers, I go back to my days at the Trump Hotel Collection and what I learned from Mr. Trump. He may be disliked by many, but his pillars of success are tried and true. They worked for him as a businessman, an entertainer, and as a candidate for the presidency.

Chapter 1 Endnotes

[1] Rebecca Muller, "What Lady Gaga's Oscar Speech Taught Us About Pursuing Your Dreams," *Thrive News,* February 25, 2019.

[2] Ibid.

[3] John Dean, *The Preposterous Success Story of America's Pillow King,* www.bloomberg.com/news/features/2017-01-11/the

[4] "Michael J. Lindell," *Wikipedia, The Free Encyclopedia*

[5] "My Pillow Founder Mike Lindell: Donald Trump was 'chosen by God' to run for president," https://www.washingtontimres.com/news/2019/mar/1/mike-lindell-my-pillow-founder-says-donald-trump-w/

[6] Ibid.

[7] David Rothman, "The Story of the My Pillow King," *CBS News.* Retrieved 24 October 2018.

[8] "Inspiring Views Above the Noise," Maria Shriver, https://mailchi.mp/mariashriver/what-are-you-great-at-sunday-paper?e=15aaeed9b7

[9] "Peace Corps," *Wikipedia, The Free Encyclopedia*

[10] "The Founding Moment," President John F. Kennedy's University of Michigan Speech, Michigan Union, Ann Arbor, October 14, 1960.

[11] "History of Special Olympics," https://www.SODE.ORG/ABOUT/

[12] Oct. 2007 Press Release to announce Trump Hotels

[13] Excerpted from "Passion Capital: The World's Most Valuable Asset," 2012, Paul Alofs, interview for "8 Rules for Creating a Passionate Work Culture"

[14] Roger Stone, *The Making of the President 2016: How Donald Trump Orchestrated a Revolution*, (New York: Skyhorse, 2017.)

Chapter Two

Drive – Get Up and Get Going
Staying in Neutral is Not an Option

People who are driven set high goals and expect much of themselves and others

~ Donald J. Trump

McShane & Von Glinow[1] wrote about the seven competencies that are characteristic of effective leaders, and drive is one of them. Mr. Trump's no holds barred management style drives him to get things done. It is not for the faint of heart! After answering in the affirmative when people ask me if I have met Mr. Trump, I usually get this follow-up question: "Is he the same in person as he is on TV?" My response is "What you see is what you get." What is it about this man who is so driven that he used those skills to get elected to the presidency? Some say it is partly because he has an overwhelming fear of failure.

I believe it fair to say that for decades what drove people to work hard was the ability to support themselves and their families with a paycheck and the hope of a pension at retirement age. People in my parents' generation pursued jobs at places where other family members worked, usually in the same town. Often, if you had a family member working in an auto plant, you got hired in that same plant. Automobile factories, mining, and other manufacturing jobs could have two or three generations of families all working together in the same place. It was not uncommon back then for someone to spend an entire career in the same job at the same company. Today, things are different. Many more choices exist, people are more mobile, more educated, and typically less loyal. What drives people today is more about doing what they love and having flexibility and feeling empowered. Companies should spend more time finding out what drives employees to do a great job, and then make the necessary investment in human capital.

From an early age Mr. Trump enjoyed the building industry, and even more so the real estate piece of it. His father, Fred Trump, was a builder of apartment buildings in several of the boroughs of New York. To make him more disciplined, his parents sent young Trump to military school, where he became a star athlete. He began his college education at Fordham University in New York, and then transferred to the University of Pennsylvania's Wharton School of Business. After graduating in 1968, Donald Trump went to work for his father. He said, "My father was my mentor, and I learned a tremendous amount about every aspect of the construction industry from him."

About five years or so after this, Donald Trump began acquiring some of the most exclusive and expensive real estate in New York City. As time went on and he was making money, he purchased the Plaza Hotel in New York, in a bidding war, for $390 million. When the Plaza originally opened in 1907, it was a 250-foot tall building extending along Central Park and Fifth Avenue. To me, it is the finest location in New York City – simply iconic, then and now. In 1988 Trump purchased the property from Westin Hotels (my employer at the time), and I was especially intrigued to see what he planned for this great lady. A former boss of mine worked at the Plaza when Trump bought it. One of my (six) brothers worked as a busboy in the legendary Edwardian Room where the waiters, many of whom were in their sixties, had all worked for decades. My brother had wait staff experience, but getting a job there meant starting out as a busboy and working your way up. Generally, that took years, as it typically meant someone literally had to die for an opening to come up. On purchasing the Plaza, Trump said "This isn't just a building, it's the ultimate work of art. I was in love with it." His goal was to make it a five-star hotel in the first year, which is normally an unreachable goal. Trump appointed Ivana (his first wife), as the president of the hotel at a salary of

$1.00 per year and all the dresses she wanted. Knowing Ivana's love of fashion, Trump might have saved money had he just paid her a salary. She oversaw the $50 million renovation he embarked upon to bring the Plaza back to its original grandeur. Unfortunately, the Trumps did not receive the five-star ranking they so desired.

A few years into Trump's ownership, he and Ivana divorced, and that set him back financially. In November 1992 Trump filed for bankruptcy protection for the Plaza, as the hotel could no longer meet its debt obligations. A month later, a federal bankruptcy judge approved a plan for Citibank and other lenders to sell Mr. Trump's prized possession. This is a prime example of a successful initial endeavor that turned into failure. In 1995, the Plaza was sold for $325 million to a partnership between Prince Alwaleed bin Talal of Saudi Arabia and CDL Hotels International of Singapore. Mr. Trump did not receive any proceeds. Even with the loss of money and his prized possession gone, Trump said, "One of the great deals was the Plaza, because way beyond the price, I was able to get favors from the banks and from others."[2] This speaks to Mr. Trump's second pillar of success, drive. Although he lost the Plaza, his drive set him on a mission to build and develop other real estate projects. He has the drive to be unconventional in any role he takes on. People like him set high goals, are driven to meet them, and expect others to do the same. Corporations that are mission-driven can and do accomplish amazing results. And they do so with employees who have the drive to meet or exceed the expectations that are set for them. Individuals who are driven can and often do achieve remarkable results.

Oprah Winfrey was born into abject poverty, to a single teenage mother in Mississippi when segregation still existed.

After becoming pregnant at 14 and losing her premature baby, she was sent to Tennessee to live with her father. During high school she took a job in a radio station, and that became the impetus that drove her to secure a better life for herself than what she experienced as a young girl. She worked her way up, doing local news and eventually starting her own daytime talk show that ran from 1986-2011 and was loved by millions. She has since parlayed into acting, producing, and authoring, and created her own production company as well. It is reported that her wealth as of January 2019 is $2.6 billion. The University of Illinois taught a course focusing on her business acumen entitled "History 298: Oprah Winfrey, The tycoon." Oprah is known around the globe and admired by people from all walks of life. Her drive to succeed is evident in her business life as well as in her personal life. She is highly regarded for her drive to help others accomplish their goals – from funding the Oprah Winfrey Leadership Academy for Girls in South Africa to donating to Project Cuddle, which rescues babies that are abused and abandoned. She donates millions to three foundations: The Angel Network, The Oprah Winfrey Foundation, and the Oprah Winfrey Operating Foundation. The Winfrey Foundation is funded by an endowment and individuals can donate to it. Oprah's will include a provision for donating one billion dollars to charity.[3]

Oprah is the epitome of the American dream. She is a self-made millionaire – no one gave her anything; she worked tirelessly for years pursuing a career to achieve all that she has and everything that she has accomplished. Oprah did not inherit wealth like Trump or John Kennedy. Both men, with varying degrees of financial security, could have sat on their laurels and lived off their inheritance and interest income; yet, they were, like Oprah, driven to do more, and both ultimately were chosen to lead our nation as president.

I cannot imagine that even his biggest critics would not admit that Donald J. Trump possesses drive and energy, even if they perceive his drive as a negative quality. Judge Jeanine Pirro, a friend of the president for decades, often speaks about his boundless energy. He requires that people who work for him be energetic and use their drive to be successful. Several of his cabinet members, a few younger than he by decades, say Trump has more energy than they. Mr. Trump was driven to start a luxury hotel company that has grown and prospered. He strategically selected cities in which to build, and each property had a construction timeline which Mr. Trump was driven to meet or exceed. In the first presidential debate, with a record 80 million people tuned in, Trump at one point told the audience that his Washington, D.C. hotel was ahead of schedule and under budget, which was what he expected of all projects. The reference was meant to speak to his financial acumen and ability to run a company, which the majority of politicians have not done.

During his speech at the Republican National Committee winter meeting on February 1, 2018, he paraphrased himself from the previous day's State of the Union address, when he mentioned the Empire State Building being constructed in one year. For his buildings, coming in ahead of schedule and under budget saved hundreds of thousands of dollars – money that could be used later for property improvements.

My youngest sibling, Nicole, was born at 26 weeks when our Mom was 44 years old. Unlike today, in those days very premature babies did not have good chances for survival. Nicole weighed less than three pounds and was in intensive care for a few months. I remember seeing her for the first time, the day after she was born. Although her fragile body was slight, she had the most beautiful face and jet-black hair. Her entire body could fit in the palm of my hand. She remained in the hospital until she reached a weight of around five pounds or so, which allowed her to come home. As a toddler she would place her hands into my shoes and walk with her body on the ground. When it was obvious that she could not walk upright, at about two years old, she was diagnosed with cerebral palsy. In those days, 45 years ago, much less was known about and little help given to children with CP, even though it is the most common childhood disability.

Nicole's drive to be like the other kids, despite the awkward stares and insensitive questions, gave her the means to succeed. She graduated from college, became an author, blogger, and CP advocate. She has devoted much of the last five years, since undergoing a surgical procedure that has significantly changed her life, to CP advocacy. She embarked upon a campaign in 2019 to get one building in each of our 50 states to light up in green (CP's color) on National CP Day, March 25. Not only did she reach her goal – she exceeded it by getting more than 100 buildings/landmarks/hotels in all 50 states and Canada to light up. Some of the buildings include the Helmsley Hotel in New York, Ford Field in Detroit, the Wrigley Building in Chicago and the Space Center in Houston. Nicole's drive to bring CP, which affects 17 million children and adults worldwide, out of the shadows, is what made this possible. Does she get rejections or no response from people and organizations? Yes, without a doubt. But she is determined, focused, and driven to make a difference, and she has done so. Nicole will tell you she is just one person without fame or name recognition – but with the drive to make a difference, thereby proving that one person can have an impact.

Because of his drive Trump has done things that have nothing to do with his business. On February 12, 2018, in a meeting about infrastructure, Trump mentioned the Wollman Rink in New York City as an example of getting things done. It had been sitting vacant for years and no one could figure out how to make it functional. He was interested in resurrecting it as it was a beloved location for children and their parents to skate. According to Wikipedia, the rink was closed in 1980 for a proposed two years of renovations at a cost of $9.1 million. Six years after the problem-plagued work had still not been completed by the city, Donald Trump persuaded Mayor Ed Koch to let him finish the job. Koch initially objected, but relented and allowed Trump to take on the challenge. Trump completed the renovations in four months. Trump did what he said, in record time and at a final cost 25 percent below the budget and for no profit. The rink reopened to the public on November 13, 1986.

Mr. Trump's drive was evident to me when I went to Trump Tower to film our employee orientation video, which included footage of Mr. Trump, the Trump kids, our CEO, VP of marketing, and me. As we waited for Mr. Trump, Eric Trump was being filmed as he spoke into the camera from the cue cards we had prepared in advance. It struck me how this young man, then all of 22 years old, was mature, poised, and proud. The confidence he portrayed and the manner in which he spoke commanded attention. He did his part and quietly exited the room. Then Mr. Trump entered (the same room where The Apprentice was filmed) accompanied by his bodyguard Keith Schiller. He went directly to the chair in front of the camera, sat down and said something like "Let's go, I have ten appointments today." He proceeded to read his script (which I co-authored) and he did his part in two takes, reading from the teleprompter. It took all of about ten minutes and he was gone. The last line of the script, my favorite, was when he said to the new employees, "Congratulations, you're hired!" We were expecting Mr. Trump to chat with us for a few minutes; however his schedule did not permit him to do so.

He was no different on the phone. People basically had to pitch whatever they had to offer, and do it quickly. He had no time or patience for a long, drawn out presentation. He speaks on this very topic when he tells the story of hiring a very bright, qualified young man who he thought was going to be great. He then says, "Was I ever wrong. He took so long to explain anything that every time I saw him, I began to dread any kind of interaction with him."[4] Whenever the COO needed me to compile information, which often included preparing spreadsheets and detailed statistics, he would usually condense or rework the information to make it more succinct for Mr. Trump. The bottom line is this: Mr. Trump is driven to get the best deal, and the financial aspect is most important. From everything I've read and what I know from working for the Trump Organization, I believe that Mr. Trump got some of his drive from his father. And he was driven to be even better and bigger than his dad.

On the campaign trail, Trump was driven to go to as many states as possible. It didn't matter if the state was small or large or red or blue. He was driven to get up early and attend as many rallies as possible in a single day. He often talked about how he could go all day and night and speak to thousands of people while the media traveling with him was so exhausted.

His ego drives both the excitement with which he does things and his lifestyle. On the other hand, his overwhelming fear of failure and losing his status also drives him. In a *New York Times* article published weeks before the election it was stated that Trump "is intoxicated by the glow of his name in the news media."[5] By the time he was an established businessman, Mr. Trump hired a service to compile the swelling number of references to him in the media; thousands a day. The article went on to say that Trump quickly figured out that the media attention was free advertising. This led him to frequently participate in newspaper and television interviews. Trump has a drive to be different – and this was quite evident to me on the campaign trail. He chastised the press at every opportunity, such as when they did not show the crowds at his rallies. He coined the phrase "fake news" when something was said or reported that he did not agree with. And as president this drive to be different has only continued, and on a daily basis, including most notoriously his use of Twitter. No candidate, no president in history has used the media and social media as he has done.

He is in part successful, I believe, because he is not a politician. He speaks like many of us wish we could if not for the consequences, such as losing one's job. In my dealings with the Trump Organization, it was my experience that Mr. Trump had a drive to be right no matter what the topic, and particularly if it involved his holdings and his wealth. He has sued reporters who did not refer to him as a billionaire in articles about his financial status and wealth. When the media did their fact-checking and noted any error, Trump typically came back with his usual retort that he was misquoted or taken out of context. We've all worked with people and bosses who want either to be right or at least have the last word. That trait can be a slippery slope, an advantage, or not so advantageous depending upon how, where, and when it is utilized.

Mr. Trump the businessman also had the drive to make his hotels the best with the ultimate in service. He understood that happy employees make for satisfied and loyal guests. When the 2008 recession hit within weeks of the Las Vegas property opening, we had to make some tough decisions – decisions in which the Trumps were directly involved. After determining what was required to sustain keeping the hotel afloat and how many employees would be affected, the conversations with the Trumps began. I had personally worked with and hired dozens of the employees who were ultimately impacted, so it was a very emotional time for me.

Even though most of the employees had only been on the payroll for a month, we wanted to do something for them. Many had given up good jobs where they had seniority, so I felt obligated to let the Trump kids know we should offer a financial award, and they gave us the green light to do so. Each affected employee received severance, and we paid for their continued healthcare for up to several months depending upon their length of employment. The overall financial impact was not small, but it was the right thing to do! I always appreciated that Don Jr., Ivanka, and Eric took the recommendation and got it approved by their dad. So, when people say Mr. Trump does not care about the average Joe, I do not agree. He also, without any fanfare, assists those in need. During training, before the Las Vegas opening, one of our employees died in a motorcycle accident. Mr. Trump wanted to assist the family. Most of the Las Vegas crew attended the funeral, and afterward we hosted a celebration of life reception at the hotel. Mr. Trump does have a heart; however, I think he doesn't display it in a way that his critics deem acceptable. I know that prior to becoming president he and his organization were asked by people and entities such as nonprofits for donations, sponsorships, and in-kind contributions. There are so many in so much need, and I saw firsthand that the Trump Organization was philanthropic. The most visible to me was Eric Trump. I attended an event at Trump's golf course in Bedminster, New Jersey, hosted by Eric and his then girlfriend (now wife), Lara, for St. Jude Children's Hospital. There were famous people in attendance, including the baseball player Darryl Strawberry. The event raised millions of dollars for St. Jude's. That same year, at the Christmas holidays, hotel employees at the Trump properties asked guests when they checked in if they wished to donate to St. Jude. I was pleasantly surprised at the participation we received.

The drive that Mr. Trump has was instilled in his kids, and I witnessed it up close and personal. They were often at their desks working well past 6:00 pm, when others had already left the building. They were driven, like their father, to be the best at whatever they did. Mr. Trump taught his kids the value of money and made sure they worked for it. They were driven to please their dad, who was not simply their father but also their boss. Growing up in an affluent family, attending some of the finest schools and being parented by successful individuals does not always lead to success in life. In the case of Mr. Trump's kids, they are as driven as he is to be successful. Again, not without failures. In early 2019, Donald Jr. and Eric Trump announced they were dissolving plans for two hotel branded companies they had announced after their dad's inauguration.

I believe President Trump's drive permeates his behavior in global affairs. He is driven to go down in history as one of the best American presidents. He, like most leaders, has an ego and that comes through loud and clear. His drive to meet with foreign leaders, friends and foes alike, is played out in his tweets, in newsworthy events, at cabinet meetings, and in press conferences. He is driven to broker peace in the Middle East, to have a positive relationship with Vladimir Putin of Russia, and to engage Kim Jong Un, the president of North Korea. Trump loves to be the first to do something, and the meeting in June of 2018 with Kim Jong Un was indeed historic. To protect his image and keep his promise to the American people, he gave a caveat regarding the meeting, saying, "If I think that it's a meeting that is not going to be fruitful, we're not going to go. If the meeting, when I'm there, is not fruitful, I will respectfully leave the meeting."[6] The second summit with Kim Jong Un in Hanoi, the city of peace, took place in February, 2019, and was cut short as no deal was reached. President Trump invoked the words of President Reagan in speaking to the press, saying that no deal is better than a bad deal. Whether he is successful or not going forward is up for debate and history will, of course, decide.

In her book about four of our presidents, Teddy Roosevelt, Franklin Roosevelt, Abraham Lincoln and Lyndon Johnson, historian Doris Kearns Goodwin studied their leadership styles and the question if leaders are born or made. She says these four were "united by a fierce ambition, an inordinate drive to succeed."[7] I believe that can be said of most of our presidents. Unless one has drive, it is difficult to succeed at anything, let alone being president. In my estimation, and particularly given his age, President Trump leads the pack in this dimension of leadership.

Throughout my career, I've seen hundreds of examples of

people who are so driven that they accomplish whatever it is they set their mind to. Drive also takes discipline. Think for a moment about the New England Patriots and the drive that the coach (Bill Belichick) and quarterback (Tom Brady) both have to excel. Every season it seems the Patriots are breaking yet another record. The drive to win is played out in everything they do. Even if they are down by 12 points with only two minutes remaining in the fourth quarter, they are driven to win and often, against the odds, achieve that result. In February, 2019, the Patriots won another Super Bowl, their sixth under the Belichick-Brady regime. You must love what you do and do it to the best of your ability. In the workplace, employees who are driven usually contribute more and are extremely productive. Driven individuals set high goals for themselves in life and in business. It could be as simple as providing well for their families. It may include the drive to be promoted and earn more money. Drive may also include internal competition with peers, as is often seen in organized sports beginning with little league and on through college and professional sports, the Olympics, etc.

The Seattle Seahawks made NFL history when in April of 2018 they signed twin brothers Shaquem and Shaqueem Griffin, both of whom had played football at the University of Central Florida. One of the brothers, Shaqueem, was born with a syndrome affecting his left hand, with fingers on that hand not fully developed. He was in such great pain as a young boy that he tried to cut off his hand. His parents had to take him for surgery to have the hand amputated. That did not stop the young man from playing sports, including competing in track and baseball. He also played football in high school and college. Shaquem Griffin became the first one-handed player selected in the NFL draft as the fifth pick and the 141st overall. He led the Seahawks in tackles during the 2018 preseason. Shaquem says, "It was literally like a dream, like I was actually imagining stuff and it just started happening."[9] Shaqueem's popularity and the publicity he has received has given hope to children born with only one hand or arm. At a recent fan event, Shaqueem was seen greeting and holding a young boy who had only one hand. Shaqueem has said, "If I had two hands, I don't think I'd be good as I am now."[9] He is an inspiration to anyone who is disabled and shows us all that anything is possible if you possess the drive.

Think about successful business people who are out of the work force. Those who were driven in their careers and accomplished fame, stature, or financial wealth usually do not sit back and retire, as they well could. Who comes to my mind is Jack Welch, former Chief Executive Officer of General Electric. After attaining a PhD in chemical engineering, Jack joined GE in 1960, and worked his way up to CEO and chairman in 1981 (becoming their youngest chairman ever). He remained at the helm until 2001. When he retired, he received a $417 million payout, and his net worth was estimated at $720 million. Jack may have retired from GE, but not from working. He became an adviser to a private equity firm, and was active on the public-speaking circuit. He and his wife Suzy co-wrote columns for *Businessweek* for four years, until in 2009 he founded the Jack Welch Management Institute. Jack published his book, *Winning,* co-authored with Suzy, about management, and it soared to #1 on *The Wall Street Journal* bestseller list. He went on to teach a course at the Massachusetts' Institute of Technology Sloan School of Management to a group of MBA students. In 2016, Welch was part of a business group that provided strategy, policy, and economic advice to president-elect Donald Trump. Mr. Welch, now 83 years old, is still going strong with a net worth of approximately $750 million.[15] He was driven in business and still has the drive to continue being successful in whatever he embarks upon.

Mentoring is an excellent way to assist those employees who you believe have potential and possess the drive to do more. Over the years I worked with and developed numerous formal mentoring programs consisting of applications, interviews, and requirements for both mentors and mentees, expectations for both, plus assignments and reporting mechanisms. Many organizations have such programs, as do colleges and universities. SCORE (Service Corps of Retired Executives), is the nation's largest network of volunteer business experts. This non-profit, supported by the US Small Business Administration, started in 1964. Score's goal is to help one million clients by 2020. There are invaluable resources to help businesses get started, grow, and achieve their goals through education and mentorship. Score has more than 300 chapters all over the country and offers mentorships, in-person workshops, and on-line webinars and resources. Public libraries are another resource often providing free seminars, talks, and information on many topics to help people become more successful in their personal and/or business lives. For those who are determined, dedicated and driven, there is plenty of help out there.

The buddy system is a different approach to assist those employees who may need a boost with drive. Placing your best employees, those seen by their peers as informal leaders, with those that you want to improve (whether in terms of their passion, drive, or enthusiasm), can be extremely effective. It takes time, patience, and leadership to create and maintain this type of program. Employees selected as mentors or buddies should receive recognition and gratitude. Start each program with a celebration of those selected, and along the way hold meetings and other events to both train and reward the participants. Give them recognition in newsletters, meetings, social media and whatever other communication vehicles are available. We know that Mr. Trump had at least one mentor – his father, Fred, whom he credits for much of his success. Trump returned the favor and mentored Don Jr, Ivanka, and Eric. For all of his traits, both good and bad, they have learned much at his hands and are each successful in their own right. Parents should, at an early age, use similar mentoring techniques with their own children. It is far easier to teach traits and skills early on rather than later.

Success does not look the same for every person or in every occupation. It does not always include wealth or recognition. The world is full of everyday people toiling at teaching or farming or research who achieve their version of success. One individual I know personally is Dr. Jason Comander, a physician and researcher studying and conducting clinical trials with those that have degenerative eye diseases, particularly retinitis pigmentosa (RP). Dr. Comander is a soft-spoken, young, Harvard-trained researcher at Massachusetts Eye & Ear Infirmary (MEEI), a world-renowned hospital. Because of his drive to do research and find a cure, he works mainly behind the scenes. I'm sure he could have gone into private practice earning more money than what he currently earns. But, for Dr. Comander, the chance to work on something that could be revolutionary drives him to keep doing the work. In 2018, he transplanted stem cells into the eyes of a New Jersey teenager who was blind as a result of RP. That young man has his sight today thanks to

Dr. Comander. In late 2018, that teenager's story was featured on national television. Dr. Comander's name was not mentioned in the coverage, because the focus was on the boy. I felt compelled to tweet about it and mention Dr. Comander as an example of success in the field of medical research. His drive to restore vision in those who have little or no sight and to find a cure is unparalleled.

When discussing drive and teaching about it, in order to get students or business folks engaged in the process, ask these questions:

- Who do you know, or admire, that is driven?

- Tell us how you see "drive" as a trait manifested in that person?

- What drives YOU to wake up in the morning?

- What drives YOU to come to work/volunteer every day?

- What drives YOU to do a good job (whether it is a paid job or volunteering)?

- What drives YOU to meet or exceed expectations?

- What drives YOU to help your co-workers, family, community?

For folks who may answer any of these questions but not exhibit drive themselves, the follow-up questions could be:

- What would it take at work (or school), to become more driven?

- How can we (at work or school), help you to feel more drive to do better (with grades, productivity, etc.).

Answers and suggestions to these and other questions will enable the facilitators/teachers/professors to follow-up with subsequent discussions and keep the process going.

Chapter 2 Endnotes

[1] Steven McShane and Mary M.Von Glinow, *Organizational Behavior,* (New York: McGraw-Hill, 2010).

[2] David Seal, "What Donald Trump's Plaza Deal Reveals About His White House Bid," *The New York Times,* January 16, 2016.

[3] www.oprahwinfrey.com, https://www.looktothestarts.org/celebrity/oprah

[4] Donald J. Trump with Meredith McIver, *Think Like a Champion*, (New York: Vanguard Press, 2009)
2016.

[5] Scott Lucas, *World View Trump Watch, 454*: "Trump Gives Himself an Exit from Meeting with North Korea's Kim," April 19, 2018.

[6] Doris Kearns Goodwin, *Leadership: In Turbulent Times,* (New York: Simon & Schuster, 2018.)

[7] Michael Middlehurst-Schwartz, *USA Today*, "Shaquem Griffin drafted by Seahawks, becomes first-one handed player picked in NFL draft modern era," April 28, 2018, https://www.usatoday.com/story/sports/nfl/drft/shaquem-griffin-seattle-seahawks-nfl-draft-pick-history-hand-558751002/

[8] Jared Dubin, CBSN Live, November 15, 2018. https://www.cbssports.com>60minutes>60minutessports

[9] "Jack Welch," *Wikipedia,* https://en.wikipedia.org/wiki/Jack_Welch

Chapter 3

Enthusiasm – What Excites You?
Make America Great Again (MAGA)

Enthusiasm is the most important thing in life
                                        ~ Tennessee Williams

I think that Donald Trump, who admires Winston Churchill, would agree with Churchill's statement that "success is the ability to go from one failure to another with no loss of enthusiasm." Enthusiasm, for Mr. Trump, starts with him. Whether it is a business meeting where he will boast to others about his worth, his holdings, or his properties, or now, as president, about how much he has done for America, he is genuinely enthusiastic about himself and life. That enthusiasm translates into his attitude toward business, golf, and with his "Make America Great Again" mantra. He has repeatedly told the world that he is a winner (even when he loses), and that fuels his enthusiasm.

I personally witnessed his enthusiasm when he came to Las Vegas for the May, 2007 topping off ceremony. Trump's confidence and bravado in front of his fans and supporters was unwavering. His enthusiasm helps to keep him vital and relevant. Back then he was barely 60 years old, and anyone who saw him remarked about his endless energy and enthusiasm. Today, at 72 years young, nothing has changed, and in fact it seems as if his energy has doubled. I imagine winning the presidential election can boost one's energy. Candidate Trump regularly spoke about the word "enthusiasm" at his rallies, typically using it against his Democratic opponent. He would comment on how enthusiastic his crowds were, and that we didn't see enthusiasm like that at a Hillary rally. Niall Stanage, a professor who has given many lectures about Trump, noted in an article, "One reason for his strength: people who intend to vote for him are more enthusiastic about doing so than those planning to back Clinton."[1] He goes on to say in the article that Clinton did not ignite enthusiasm and Donald Trump was much more adept at doing so.

For me, it is no wonder that Mr. Trump heralded enthusiasm as the third of his three pillars of success. Today, on various websites for Trump-branded businesses, including the Trump Hotels recruiting page, employees will speak about one or all of his pillars. The employees are part of the Trump Brand culture. There is no room in his hotels for whiners or losers, as Mr. Trump refers to them. Mr. Trump's enthusiasm can be seen in his facial expressions, tone of voice, and the words that he chooses when interacting with guests or supporters. He approaches life with enthusiasm and it shows in everything that he does. Any corporation lacking enthusiastic employees can learn "Trump Talk "and how making enthusiasm part of the culture makes for a better company. Just watching Trump's facial expressions and body language will pretty well tell you what he is thinking.

One of the most enthusiastic people I admire is Kim Gravel, a woman who currently sells a line of clothing and beauty products on the shopping channels. My sister, who is a huge fan and customer of Kim's, told me of her and how she connects with her customers. So I decided to do some research on this unknown (to me) woman. Kim radiates enthusiasm about life, her products and her customers. She has a tremendous spirit and it shows in everything she does. Kim also personally connects with members of her audience by posting photos on Instagram and Facebook of them wearing her clothes and make-up. She enthusiastically responds to inquiries and comments and she gets it that her customers have contributed greatly to her success. At age 19, she was selected as the youngest Miss Georgia and represented her state in the Miss America pageant. After her pageant days, Kim served as a US goodwill ambassador to Japan. Kim then launched a career as a singer and songwriter and, building on her success, in 2009 she created "Belle Beauty" after working as a make-up artist for Dior. Her clothing line, "Belle," was introduced in 2016. Using her pageant knowledge and experience, she started a TV show, "Kim of Queens" with her mother and sister in 2014. Kim has 52,000 followers on Instagram and was seen regularly on the Steve Harvey Show. She is a life coach and is sought after as a motivational speaker. Kim's enthusiasm and love for life in all that she does is a prime example of using that skill to her benefit.

Prior to the opening of two Trump Hotels properties in 2008 we were doing our research in all areas (room rates, wage rates, and so on) for what was our comp set (the hotels in our area that would be considered our competition). When it was time to actually set the room rates, we considered our competition the luxury and high-end properties on the strip, like the Venetian and the Bellagio, so we recommended room rates in that comp set. The Trumps were confident that guests would book our hotel and pay those rates. Mr. Trump, of course, who praised everything about his property as fantastic or the best, was enthusiastic when he heard this news. However, when the recession hit a month or so after our opening, it was, sadly, a different story for us and indeed for all of the country. However, we enthusiastically rode out the recession and carried on.

During the early stages of the road to the nomination, no other candidate had the enthusiasm of Donald J. Trump. Like him or despise him, the seventy-year-old guy had bravado, a swagger, an air about him that bolstered his self-confidence. The qualities just mentioned, as well as his enthusiasm, brought millions of people into his base. I'm confident that many of his volunteers signed up because they were similarly enthusiastic. In fact, on the "Citizens for Trump" website, the first sentence stated, "Citizens for Trump is looking for **enthusiastic** volunteers to help coordinate, plan, promote, and execute strategies." Tori Richards wrote an article about speaking to several volunteers, including one from Alaska, a state with only three electoral votes. The gentleman told her, "I have to do something. I was losing sleep over it."[2] Ms. Richards noted that "voter enthusiasm is a factor – and the Trump campaign points to the energy of its supporters." Interestingly, many of the folks who became Trump campaign volunteers aggressively pursued the opportunity rather than being called upon to volunteer.

I believe that most people want to be enthusiastic and energized about life, a cause they believe in, or a person they admire. And for many volunteering for the Trump campaign made them more enthusiastic about winning. Thousands of volunteers worked tirelessly, sometimes in extreme weather conditions, with little recognition and no pay. Even after it came to light that the Trump campaign required volunteers to sign a nondisclosure agreement, one that went far beyond a typical NDA, it did not seem to matter. In the NDA volunteers were forbidden to disparage Trump, his family members, any of his businesses or products, or his campaign. (It was the same way in his business. All of us signed a multi-page confidentiality agreement including non-disclosure, no disparagement, etc.) The volunteers truly were the people who helped make his campaign great. And at his rallies the mere mention of a thank you to the volunteers fueled their enthusiasm. In the preface to his revised version of *"Crippled America,"*[3] he noted that "the crowds were unbelievable. The enthusiasm was based on pure love and love of what we were doing." And, in speaking of his personal enthusiasm in the same book, Mr. Trump says, "I'm an unstoppable force when I'm excited." It was that same way with Trump Hotel Collection employees.

Whether in Las Vegas, Toronto, or Panama, during our meetings while the properties were under construction, enthusiasm showed on the faces of the employees, some of whom were embarking on a new career. And when we announced that one of the Trumps was going to visit a property, the enthusiasm increased. I remember when I went to Panama for a few days during the pre-opening. We were holding a press conference for the media, dignitaries, and other invited guests. The newly-appointed general manager was introduced by the Trump Organization's chief operating officer, and the Trump kids were in attendance. Their comments and remarks to media, guests, and employees showed their enthusiasm for the project – which was the first one built outside of the U.S. under the Trump Hotel Collection brand. After the remarks to the press, invited guests were taken on a tour of the property – including, of course, the exquisite guest rooms. The idea, obviously, was to get the press and other influential people excited about the property. I was impressed with the ability of Mr. Trump's kids to navigate the environment so professionally, to speak with such confidence and skill about the Panama project and the company. The apples do not fall far from the trees.

When the Las Vegas property opened, both Mr. Trump and his partner in the venture, Phil Ruffin, had a penthouse on the top floor. As is always the case with owners, it was hectic and stressful to prepare for their arrival. In the case of Mr. Trump, we had time to prepare because he was traveling from another city. Each and every corner of the property was inspected, cleaned, and re-inspected. His penthouse was in impeccable condition and only our best employees were assigned to care for it. Once those employees were chosen, the enthusiasm they had for their jobs only increased. For the very first visit by Mr. Trump, the property was so new that everything sparkled. We as a team took great pride in greeting him. I'll never forget that on his first visit after the property opened, the guest room attendant was given a gratuity by Mr. Trump, along with some very kind words. That employee often spoke with me and others about what that day and Mr. Trump's words meant to her. Trump is known for not carrying cash in his wallet, so I'm sure the tip was planned in advance, but nonetheless it made a great impression on the employees.

We were able to hire employees willing to take a step back in their career just to work for Trump and have that on their resume. Others whom we hired received promotions. One such individual was Joe Isidori. Joe was a young man in his early twenties who had graduated from culinary school, and his mother worked for the Trump Organization. He told me the story of how he was originally hired by Mr. Trump. His mother happened to mention to Trump that Joe had graduated from the Culinary Institute of America. Joe related that one morning when he was asleep, the phone rang and the call was from the Trump Organization, inviting him for an interview. Initially Joe thought he was dreaming, but he immediately decided to get dressed and go to Trump Tower.

Before he knew it, he was offered the job as Mr. Trump's chef at Mar-a-Lago. Joe was loyal to Mr. Trump and his family and he did a good job, so in the winter of 2007 he was tapped for the role of executive chef at Trump Las Vegas. The recession hit at the same time the property opened and Joe left Trump and

Las Vegas shortly thereafter to move back to his hometown, New York. He worked at a few places as executive chef before opening his own restaurant. Joe is truly an enthusiastic chef and businessman. He happens to be extremely animated and demonstrative. He has utilized his enthusiasm about making the best burgers and shakes on the planet into a global enterprise, Black Tap Craft Burgers & Beers. Joe's fame has skyrocketed – he's been on *Fox and Friends* and *Good Morning America,* and it gives me a sense of pride and enjoyment that he is doing so well. Mr. Trump hired Joe when Joe was in his early twenties, single and just starting his culinary career. Today, Joe owns restaurants all over the world, is married and a father. I'm sure he will be telling stories to his son about working for the man who became president.

Mr. Trump's enthusiasm for everything that he campaigned on has increased since he took office. Each time he goes on a trip to speak about veterans, tax reform, or something else he cares deeply about, the crowd size fuels his enthusiasm. It's like he's on the campaign trail again. Like no president before him, he has generated and continues to generate enthusiasm with his base and his new supporters. When President Trump signed the Veterans Accountability and Whistleblower Protection Act in June, 2017, he said, "The enthusiasm for the Veterans Administration and for making it right for our veterans has been incredible." In a speech for his first Thanksgiving as president, he spoke about how well the economy was doing and how much enthusiasm he saw in the American people. Given the fact that the economy has rebounded, the unemployment rate is the lowest in 50 years, African-American unemployment is at an all-time low and the stock market keeps hitting record highs, I am not at all surprised that President Trump is enthusiastic.

For example, what other president actively campaigned for the next presidential election so early in his term?

I'd like to imagine what our country would be like if every man and woman had a level of enthusiasm that matched President Trump's. They could use that energy to volunteer, to help children read, to minister to those who have fallen by the wayside, to visit the infirmed in nursing homes, and so on. It harkens back to a time in America when, under President Kennedy's leadership, Congress created the Peace Corps. That is why I believe some pundits on television speak about Trump's former status as a Democrat. Both parties have platforms and ideas we can relate to and take pride in as Americans. Unfortunately, whatever the topic, be it immigration, or guns, or something else controversial, it becomes partisan and both sides keep swiping at each other to the detriment of getting things done. Despite Democrats like Chuck Schumer and Nancy Pelosi and Republicans like Lindsay Graham and Kevin McCarthy often asking the other side to be bipartisan, the narrative never seems to change.

Enthusiastic individuals are fun to be around. In a business environment they are typically the cheerleaders, the employees that leaders want to help sell a product, a service or even a new policy. One of the most enthusiastic people I know is a former realtor of mine, Tori Harrison. Tori is a petite woman with a big personality. She looks, speaks, and exudes enthusiasm. In all of my interactions with her – in person, by phone, or in texts and emails, she is always enthusiastic and uses words that match her enthusiasm. I believe it has helped her tremendously in her business and she is one of the top agents in her area. Her company gives a portion of all sales to three charities that Tori supports. Tori's enthusiasm brings clients to her, something which is a huge advantage in any business. In addition, her enthusiasm rubs off on others, and she gets clients excited about buying or selling a home. It is far more difficult to acquire new customers than to maintain existing ones. And, in real estate, referrals are worth their weight in gold. In addition, Tori just makes it fun just to do business with her.

Not surprisingly, Mr. Trump is enthusiastic about himself. He often talks about himself in the third person. When speaking as a business leader, he has said "If you don't have the motivation and the enthusiasm, your great idea will simply sit on top of your desk or inside your head and go nowhere." During his first year as president he mentioned "the enthusiasm and spirit on every single index is higher than it's ever been before ... job enthusiasm and manufacturing, business enthusiasm is [sic] at record levels." He knows how to use words that elicit strong responses (both positive and negative) from the electorate, and everything he says gets covered each day on every news network.

On the campaign trail Trump was enthusiastic about many issues, but particularly immigration, which was a major part of his platform. In one speech he told a crowd that "we will build a great wall along the southern border and Mexico will pay for the wall."[4] At every rally, in every interview, in every small town or big city, he echoed his enthusiasm for border security, building the wall and making Mexico pay for it. His supporters bought it hook, line, and sinker. President Trump, as late as August 21, 2018, in a rally in West Virginia, told the crowd when speaking about the need to secure our borders that the wall had been started and will be built. The crowd enthusiastically cheered and shouted, "Build the wall!"

Of course, enthusiasm in politics does not always translate into success, and border security in terms of a wall has not materialized the way the president envisioned. Some say that his re-election is in doubt if the promise of building the wall is not fulfilled.

Trump was also enthusiastic about telling the crowds of Hillary Clinton's plans, her years of public service in which she accomplished nothing, and the less than enthusiastic supporters at her rallies. He said, for example, "She's got a weak temperament. She's a weak person. I think she would make a horrible president."[5] These remarks only generated enthusiasm in his audiences and motivated him to continue doing what he was doing, which included swiping at the Democrats for the state of the country, lack of border security, MS-13 gang violence, and other issues of concern to voters.

On a personal level, Mr. Trump is enthusiastic about golf. In an article written when Mr. Trump was 63 years old and still actively pursuing business ventures, expanding his hotel brand and licensing the Trump name, the author noted that "even in trying times, the charismatic, outspoken Donald Trump manages to stay energetic and stimulated by life."[6] The article goes on to give his six secrets for maintaining his edge in life. Here are two that speak to enthusiasm.

- Relentlessly confront your fears. Trump says, "The trick is to recognize your fears and then zap them with a problem-solving attitude, faith in yourself, and hard work."

- Turn your passions into productive activities. Everyone knows Trump loves to play golf. He says that "if you can capture that kind of excitement as you age, you will never stop ... enthusiasm on a big scale equals passion."

Trump has figured out that passion and drive are part of the equation for success in business and in life, and that enthusiasm has to be in the equation. He has found a way to mix these three things together to create his version of success. It worked for him in business, it worked for him on the campaign trail, and it is keeping him front and center as the president of the United States.

Leaders have the responsibility to find out what their employees are enthusiastic about in the workplace, and then cultivate that enthusiasm. The best place to begin is by identifying those employees in the organization who are enthusiastic. Determine what fuels their enthusiasm and how it can be duplicated. The enthusiastic employees can be tasked with helping to train new employees, or assigned as mentors to others in the company who show potential for advancement. Asking employees to do these things is a form of recognition and value. Many times, employees will accept training new hires or mentoring without any monetary compensation, simply because they feel honored to be chosen to do it. A formal program which includes requirements, performance expectations, and recognition does give more weight to such an initiative. Another element that I recommend is rehearsing the program as you would a speech, so that you get feedback and input from leaders in the organization who may become mentors. Once in place, leaders in the company are responsible for maintaining and enhancing the mentor program. The mentor program has advantages for those who are mentored, as they become candidates for promotion. From my experience, with time and success the mentoring program becomes competitive and employees clamor to take part in it. Ask any leader in a company and they will tell you about the folks who mentored them and had a huge impact on their career. Mentors are critically important in generating enthusiasm and developing enthusiastic employees!

Finally, it is often the guest or employee who is less than enthusiastic that commands all the attention. Whether the guest is irate or the employee disruptive, the situation is very time-consuming to turn around – yet it should be done. In my decades in the service industry, the one issue, besides communication, that many employees complain about is – the complainers. Leaders must find ways to get those people to be enthusiastic about their job and their company, or find a way to encourage them to work elsewhere. It is as simple as that. People who complain incessantly, who are not enthusiastic, who are not engaged, are toxic to others and to the workplace. They need to be identified and dealt with appropriately. It is the same way in life. If one surrounds oneself with people who complain, whine or are negative overall, it causes strain for all concerned. It is not healthy to be around people who negatively impact your mental well-being.

When teaching about leadership traits and why enthusiasm is important, discuss these things:

- Tell us about an experience you recently had (at a restaurant, a retail store, over the phone), in which the person assisting you was enthusiastic.

- What exactly did they do or say that showed you they were enthusiastic?

- How did that person's enthusiasm affect you?

- Describe a time when you worked for (or were taught by) someone less than enthusiastic.

- What affect did that person have on you and why?

- In your business role, why is enthusiasm vital?

- How do you show enthusiasm to your guests/customers/co-workers?

Chapter 3 Endnotes

1 *Northern Slant*, "100 Days of Trump: How the White House was Won," Kerry Corbett, April 28, 2017

[2] Fox News Politics "'Self-recruited' Trump Volunteers Break Mold for How Campaigns are Run," Tori Richards, November 3, 2016

[3] Donald J. Trump, *Crippled America* (New York: Simon & Schuster, 2015).

[4] CalThomas.com, "Trump Interview – The Transcript," June 8, 2016.

[5] "Transcript of Donald Trump's Immigration Speech," *The New York Times*, September 1, 2016.

[6] *Bottom Line Secrets*, "Donald Trump's 6 Secrets to Keeping Your Edge in Life," Published August 17, 2009.

Chapter 4

Communicating – Can You Hear Me Now?
@realdonaldtrump

To share information with others by speaking, writing, moving your body or using other signals
                                        ~ Cambridge Dictionary

In any walk of life, communication is vitally important. As a business person and now as president, what and how Mr. Trump communicates is not only seen by millions but scrutinized 24/7 on television, in print, and on social media.

When I worked for Mr. Trump, he relied on others to place calls for him. When he visited the properties, we did not see him with a cell phone, although I assume he had one. He did participate in television interviews that covered myriad topics. Mom and I would often watch him on *Larry King Live* where he would speak about, for example, his lawsuit against the City of Palm Beach concerning the size of the Mar-a-Lago flag. He often weighed in on things like the Iraq War, and offered his solutions on how to fix things. He toyed with the idea of running for the highest office in the land but, I believe, did not announce his candidacy because he was not at the time a viable candidate. He had to wait for the right moment. In fact, I remember speaking about this with Brian Baudreau, the second general manager of Trump Las Vegas during the time I was still employed by the Trump Hotel Collection. Brian, who referred to Mr. Trump as "Donald," did not believe Mr. Trump would announce his candidacy. Trump had not been married to Melania for long and their son Barron was still a toddler. I often felt sorry for them, as they lived in a bubble and had to have security protection whenever they stepped out of their residence at Trump tower. Brian, who had once been Trump's personal bodyguard and had known Mr. Trump for decades, was spot on in his belief that Trump had to wait for the right time.

I never saw an email or anything in writing to employees from Mr. Trump. At the time he had just one hotel, and he did business like a patriarch. I was told by a colleague that he went to New York to see Trump about a wage increase. They chatted for a few minutes and on the way out of the office, Mr. Trump told Ronna Graff, his assistant, to give the man the raise. My colleague did not sign anything and never saw any paperwork. When I inquired about his salary at the time he was hired in Las Vegas, I was given the figure verbally, but there was nothing in writing. Of course, those things changed as we transitioned the company to become more corporate. As the company grew, Mr. Trump's communication style at the hotels was typically by phone with the top leadership, and he was involved in all key decisions. His communication varied with the type of ownership of the property. For example, Mr. Trump owns 50 percent of the Las Vegas property, so he has a vested interest in its success. His partner, Phil Ruffin, owns the other 50 percent, and he lives in Las Vegas, so he is even more hands-on. Before Mr. Trump became a candidate for president, he and his three grown children were heavily involved in the management of the hotels.

Once the Trump Hotel Brand was created, we crafted an employee newsletter that became the template for all the properties. It included information on hotel occupancy and groups in house, as well as tips on delivering unparalleled guest service. Once we had better and more up-to-date technology, the newsletter was placed online and the employee intranet was created. It was important to us that employees in one city knew what was happening in other cities. It often happened that guests at one of the Trump hotels became guests at other Trump properties, so consistency in communication was paramount. The service standard of the week was the same at each property, as were our culture and values. Our chief operating officer, who reported directly to Mr. Trump, held weekly telephone conferences with the key leadership of each hotel. As vice president of human resources, I participated in corporate calls and attended meetings in New York that included the Trump kids. It was exciting to learn of the plans for future development and to go back to the property to share the news with employees. I marveled at the ability of the Trump kids to ask the most pertinent questions, inquire about financial matters, and give statistics on just about anything associated with a project off the top of their heads.

I think that most people would agree when I say that Mr. Trump's kids are more articulate than he is. It's a compliment to them that they just do it better. Mr. Trump's communication style is more shoot from the hip, voicing a lot of thoughts that often seem disjointed. He made grandiose statements as a businessman, often using statistics or information that many disbelieved. Mr. Trump uses adjectives that he loves such as great, fabulous, fantastic, and incredible. Since becoming president, Trump has made many linguistic gaffes. His tweets have contained grammatical errors and misspellings. He once tweeted, "Sorry, losers and haters. But my IQ is one of the highest and you all know it! Please do not feel stupid or insecure it's not your fault." Tara Golshan, in writing of Donald Trump's speaking style, quotes Geoffrey Pullum, who said, "His speech suggests a man with scattered thoughts, a short span of attention, and a lack of intellectual discipline and analytical skills."[1] Some people say that Trump's communication style is appealing to many; that he speaks like a salesman, which of course he was for many years. Others say his speech is just below the level of a sixth-grader, and that the majority of the words he uses are monosyllabic. Michael Maslansky says that Trump uses these strategies because: 1) he has a clear narrative, a master story that he sticks to; 2) he understands and taps into simple, emotional truths; 3) he speaks the language of his audience; 4) he is deliberately different from his peers in both style and approach.[2]

In sharp contrast, President Ronald Reagan was known as "the great communicator" and one of the best public speakers of our time. His acting career helped shape his leadership and communication styles. Reagan went on to become governor of California, ran and lost his first presidential bid, and was elected president when he ran the second time. "He communicated ... with a simplicity that made people believe that he truly was 'The Great Communicator.'"[3] During President Reagan's tenure, which ended in January, 1989, social media did not exist. He used the Oval Office, press conferences, and State of the Union addresses to speak to the American people. He did it in a grandfatherly, patient, and powerful way. Reagan said of his own speaking, "I never thought it was my style or the words I used. I wasn't a great communicator, but I communicated great things ... they came from the heart of a great nation."[4] One of Reagan's speechwriters noted, "He didn't say things in a big way, he said big things. Writers, reporters, and historians were in a quandary in the Reagan years."[5] Reagan was known for his brevity and concise speeches. He instructed his speechwriters "to follow this format: 'tell them what you're going to tell them, then tell them, and then tell them what you've told them.'"[6] Many of us learned in school that repetition works as an effective communication tool. Those of us old enough to remember Reagan's presidency can recite lines from some of his more famous speeches, including "Mr. Gorbachev, tear down this wall!"[7] (the famous line from a speech he gave in West Berlin on June 12, 1987). Five years before the "Tear down this wall" speech, Reagan stated, during another visit to West Berlin: "I'd like to ask the Soviet leaders one question: Why is the wall there?"[8] Twenty-five years after its construction, President Reagan said "I call upon those responsible to dismantle it (today)." [9]

President Reagan's prepared remarks were not popular with some in his administration. Reagan was willing to take a huge risk on behalf of humanity and global stability and progress, and he was successful. The wall was demolished on November 9, 1989. The historic event was captured for the entire world to see by television networks around the globe. During the first weekend alone more than 2 million people crossed into West Berlin, celebrating and chanting "Tor auf" (open the gate).[10] The reunification of Berlin and all Germany became official on October 3, 1990.

Several years earlier, in 1986, the Space Shuttle *Challenger* exploded within seconds of taking off. Millions watched it on live television. President Reagan's State of the Union address was scheduled for that evening, but he postponed it to address the *Challenger* tragedy. He did so from the Oval Office, heralding the heroism of the astronauts who perished and seeking to console the nation. President Reagan's communication style was focused on the American people; what he said to us was about us and he placed us in the forefront. He understood how to connect to an audience, and how all of us connected with one another in that time of grief for the entire nation. He always seemed to know the right words, use the correct tone and, when appropriate, how to employ a bit of humor.

After leaving office President Reagan was diagnosed with Alzheimer's disease. On November 5, 1994 the great communicator wrote a letter to the American people to inform them of the sad news. He concluded the letter by saying, "Let me thank you, the American people, for giving me the great honor of allowing me to serve as your president. When the Lord calls me home, whenever that may be, I will leave the greatest love for this country of ours and eternal optimism for its future."

Because of his lack of patience, Donald Trump does not have time for small talk and only wants to know the big picture. I never witnessed Mr. Trump ask others how they were doing or ask about their family – he isn't warm and fuzzy at all. In spite of this, the American people elected him to be our 45th president. Why? Partly, I believe, because he does speak more like the average Joe or Joanne, and he is not politically correct. Millions of people were sick and tired of listening to politicians' empty rhetoric, which was designed not to offend anyone and pandered to the lobbyists who filled their campaign coffers. Part of communicating is listening – something that we know is lacking on the part of most people. Often we are thinking about what we are going to say next, and as a result we miss out on important information. Mr. Trump, in listening to someone, will pick up on just one or two words, and he may take things out of context as he concentrates on only what he hears. He seems anxious to respond before the other person finishes, which impedes good listening. We see this play out on television when he takes questions from the media.

Listening is a special art and included in it is body language, including placement of hands and arms, eye contact, and posture. When President Trump is on television, his arms are often folded, and he does not always maintain eye contact with the person who is speaking. Some of this could be that there are many cameras in the room distracting him.

But I suspect his mind is just racing to the next thought, as he usually seems impatient. He appears to be quite adept at listening to negatives and what he calls "fake news." His ears do not miss anything that is not complimentary about him or his policies. Perhaps this is because he has a knack for listening to less positive statements, particularly from the media. His perceived lack of listening skills is exacerbated by his constant use of Twitter as a communication tool. While the president's use of Twitter can be positive, as it is instantaneous and sends his words straight to the people, he often reacts to something quickly and without having all the facts. His communication style is such that "anything goes." He is unabashed, unafraid, and unapologetic about sending tweets that are meant to embarrass, that call people names, or in some other way call out those with whom he disagrees. Millions of people do the same, so they can relate to this style of communicating.

Another aspect is his body language, which is unorthodox and has been written about by experts and non-experts alike. Jamie Deltren writes, "Trump's body language appears to be more distinct and unpredictable than his predecessors."[11] I don't think anyone would deny that Trump is a classic alpha male – from his handshakes, or his jockeying to get in front of a group when an official photo is being taken. During his February 5, 2019 State of the Union address, much was spoken and tweeted about Nancy Pelosi's body language and through it, what she was communicating. We are told that nonverbal communication is often more telling than the words we speak. In Ms. Pelosi's case, she was seated directly behind the president, and all eyes were on her. She did not maintain a poker face during his speech and she did not have to communicate verbally one word of what she was thinking.

When I watch him on television, in meetings where he is seated, often his arms are crossed with both hands hidden. Some say this depicts someone who is stressed or anxious. The most interesting thing I have read about his body language comes from Matt Jones, who writes that "Trump is actually very good to watch from a body language point of view, as there is little withholding or masking with him. The thoughts that go through his head are displayed on his face, in his posture and through his hand movements. If his hands are moving out of sync with his words, he's thinking on his feet and whatever comes out is likely to be equally out of sync. Think of the erratic way he answered many questions during the debates."[12]

I think it can be said that Trump is direct in both business and politics. People typically know where they stand with him. Once one receives the silent treatment from Trump, it is all over. Rex Tillerson, for example, had not had a recent conversation with the president when his termination was announced. That sort of thing has manifested itself time and again with the White House staff. Secretary of State Tillerson was overseas and learned in a tweet from President Trump that he had been fired. I'm certain Tillerson knew something was coming, but he should have been afforded a formal, in-person conversation with the man who hired him.

President Trump did not personally fire James Comey. After the deed was done, he took to the airwaves and Twitter to tell the world why he fired Comey. Now that Comey has published his book, we also have his side of the story. Various accounts have been given: the president's, that of former Deputy Attorney General Rod Rosenstein, and Comey's. In my opinion, there are too many people on the administration's team that speak about the issues, either via Twitter or on television. Everyone from Sara Huckabee-Sanders, Trump's press secretary, to Kellyanne Conway and others, weigh in on various issues. Often in the Trump administration two people will comment on a topic, and they are not aligned with the president's view. Press Secretary Sara Sanders does her best, and I can imagine how taxing her job must be, trying to juggle all the moving parts. When others comment or speak about topics they may not be expert in, she ends up backtracking or making what is perceived as a contradictory statement. The White House tells us they want to communicate and be transparent, but sometimes less is more. The communications people need to be consistently speaking with one voice. In every organization I have worked in or with there is one person in charge of communications. That person is the spokesperson and no one else is authorized to speak on behalf of the company. This is done for a reason. So too should this be the case for the president. Some of the chaos may result because the communications office is all over the map, while there are others outside of the office communicating on the record. The situation is complicated by the fact that the top communications spot has been held by four individuals in less than two years. High turnover can take a toll on people and the department.

Communication is one of the issues employees usually complain about. Years ago, in the days before computers, communicating with employees was typically in person or in written memos. With all of the technology we enjoy today, there is no excuse for poor communication in business. We can communicate by email, Twitter, intranet, newsletters, Facebook, cell phone, websites, and in other ways, often in many languages. Most major companies have a large communications department that handles internal and external communications, marketing, public relations, and social media. This is just how we do business today. I wonder how those who work in the White House receive communications, particularly with all of the leaks that we hear about from the West Wing. Even in business, it is sometimes difficult to keep something secret or confidential before an official announcement is made. When we decided to reduce staff at the start of the 2008 recession at Trump International Las Vegas, we had a plan and a long list of action items as well as an aggressive timeline. During the week it was business as usual, so a group of us worked on two consecutive weekends to prepare for the layoffs. It included notices, computing payroll check amounts, severance agreements, COBRA (Consolidated Omnibus Budget Reconciliation Act) paperwork and so on. By doing everything outside of the regular workweek, we were able to keep things under wraps until the actions took place. Once the layoffs started, meetings took place with the remaining staff to keep them apprised of what was going on. Often, communicating what happened is the piece that is most overlooked, and it can have tremendous negative consequences on those still employed, as they wonder what will happen to them. It is imperative to communicate to the remaining staff what took place and why, and to answer their questions.

We regularly hear from the media that some White House employees have learned about something from the media, so I wonder what the protocol is for communicating to them directly. In the present environment, things happen so quickly that communication may not be timely. If I worked there, this is something I would try to improve upon. Everyone needs to be on the same page in public, even if they are not in private.

In business we might disagree on a position or policy behind closed doors, but once a policy was put into place, we spoke to the employees with one voice. It is never a good thing for employees to hear the leaders in their company not speaking as one. In the case of President Trump, the *Washington Post* reported that in 466 days in office, the president had made 3,001 false or misleading claims. The article goes on to say that "Trump has a proclivity to repeat over and over many of his false or misleading statements."[13] For example, Trump has told the American people that the border wall is being built, yet Congress has not appropriated the money for it. The president also goes back and forth on statements he makes. During the campaign, he told us over and over again – at every speech, every rally, every debate – that he was going to build the wall and the Mexican government was going to pay for it. Months later, after his inauguration, when the reality of how things get done in Washington set in, he backed off of his promise that Mexico would pay. On the campaign trail he blasted China for stealing American jobs and manipulating their currency, yet his Trump-branded goods are made in China, and he buys building materials from that country.

Once General John Kelly became the president's chief of staff and brought some order and protocol to the White House, communications seemed for a time to become more centralized. White House staff members complained that they no longer had the ability to just walk into the president's office and speak to him. Kelly was receiving daily printouts of the president's incoming and outgoing phone calls, so that he would know to whom the president was speaking. Apparently, this did not go over well with President Trump, as CNN reported that he was using his personal cell phone, describing it as a "free-wheeling mode of operation that characterized the earliest days of his administration."[14] For General Kelly, being the gatekeeper is not unlike being an executive assistant to a CEO. That person is the CEO's conduit for information and the first line of defense. Things have changed, as Kelly has left and Trump named an interim chief of staff, Mick Mulvaney, who has relaxed the Kelly style of access to the President.

Another component of communicating is honesty. Martin Luther King, Jr. exemplified honest communication. Born in 1929 and growing up during the Great Depression, he attended high school in Atlanta in the segregated South. He was known for his public speaking skills and joined the debate team where he won first prize in his junior year. King was an honor student, graduating from high school early by skipping two grades. In addition to his passion for social justice, he traveled the country, joining protests and vigils, speaking about his dream for all Americans. In the 1960s, when segregation was still the law of the land in some places, it was difficult for MLK Jr. to gain white support for his views. He was arrested 29 times for what today would be simply asserting his right of freedom of speech. King, a Baptist minister and activist held several degrees, including a PhD in systematic theology from Boston University that he was awarded in 1955. That same year, he led the Montgomery bus boycott, which began when a black woman, Rosa Parks, refused to give up her bus seat to a white man and was arrested. The bus boycott lasted over a year and became so violent that King's home was bombed. In 1957, King and others founded the Southern Christian Leadership Conference (SCLC) to organize black churches to protest nonviolently against social injustice. By 1962, during the Kennedy presidency, King voiced concerns about the slow pace with which the administration was dealing with segregation. King called upon the president to issue an executive order along the lines of the Emancipation Proclamation. No such order followed, so King continued to promote non-violent protest on behalf of civil rights for blacks.

King continued to preach and orate, including giving series of lectures called *The American Race Crisis.* "MLK's success is greatly impacted by his many soft skills. He was an incredible orator and motivator."[15] He spoke out about and led marches for the right to vote, desegregation, housing, and labor rights. King's written and verbal communications evoked passion, determination and honesty. His cadence, tone, and word selection were masterful and those who listened hung on to his every word. Perhaps the most famous of the marches was the 1963 March on Washington, D.C. King, as part of the SCLC, joined others from six civil rights groups on August 28, 1963. President Kennedy, who initially was not a proponent of the march, thinking it would impede passage of civil rights legislation, eventually worked to ensure it was successful. Because of the administration's involvement, some of the civil rights leaders felt the march was not what they intended. However, more than a quarter of a million people attended the event which was, at the time, the largest gathering of protestors in Washington D.C.'s history.

MLK Jr. delivered his now famous "I Have a Dream" speech in approximately fifteen minutes. These lines are remembered by millions and have been re-visited for decades:

I say to you, my friends, so even though we face difficulties of today and tomorrow, I still have a dream.
It is a dream deeply rooted in the American dream.
I have a dream that one day this nation will rise up

and live out the true meaning of its creed: 'We hold these truths to be self-evident: that all men are created equal.'

I have a dream that one day on the red hills of Georgia the sons of former slave owners will be able to sit together at the table of brotherhood.

I have a dream that one day even in the state of Mississippi, a state sweltering with the heat of oppression, will be transformed into an oasis of freedom and justice.

I have a dream that my four little children will one day live in a nation where they will not be judged by the color of their skin but by the content of their character.

I have a dream today.

I have a dream that one day, down in Alabama, with its vicious racists, with its governor having his lips dripping with the words of interposition and nullification; one day right there in Alabama, little black boys and black girls will be able to join hands with little white boys and white girls as sisters and brothers.

I have a dream today.

In his short time on earth, MLK Jr. wrote five books, was

the father of five children, and left a legacy of peace through non-violence. MLK Jr. was the recipient of the Nobel Peace Prize in 1964, the same year in which the Civil Rights legislation introduced in Congress under John F. Kennedy was passed and signed into law by President Lyndon B. Johnson. Martin Luther King was assassinated in Memphis, Tennessee on April 4, 1968, at the age of 39. He was posthumously awarded the Presidential Medal of Freedom in 1977 and the Congressional Gold Medal in 2004. It took 32 years for all 50 states in our nation to observe the national holiday which President Reagan proclaimed as Martin Luther King Day in 1983. It is observed on the third Monday of January, the month of Dr. King's birth. The Reverend Dr. King spoke honestly and was murdered for speaking the truth. It was a sad day in America that is indelibly etched in our history. King communicated then what is true today and his dream still lives on.

When employees ask a question, they want an honest answer. If the answer is not known at the time, it is imperative that follow-up takes place. It is no secret that Mr. Trump has gone on the record in publications and interviews about his wealth and holdings. In order to make the Forbes 400 list over thirty years ago, Mr. Trump, it has been said, was not so honest about his personal wealth. Candidate Trump did not disclose his tax returns and during the campaign stated that he was being audited. He communicated to the American public that he would release the returns when the audit was completed. Then he switched positions and said he was not releasing his tax returns because people were not interested. While we may not have that information, we do know some things about his interests from disclosure forms he was required to complete.

President Trump is the wealthiest person to hold the

office of president. His golf courses and associated companies account for about 50 percent of the income listed, at least $308 million. In an article by Emily Stewart for *The Street* in September, 2015, Trump said, "The fact is I built a net worth of more than $10 billion." His detractors call for the president to release his financial information so the truth can be known by the American people.

We hear in the mainstream media that President Trump tells lies. His defenders see it differently. Anthony Scaramucci, former White House communications director, in a June, 2018 interview with Chris Cuomo of CNN, was asked by Cuomo, "When you lie, shouldn't you be called a liar?" To which Scaramucci responded, "Because there are different styles of communication." Cuomo quickly came back with "Lying is not a style of communication." I personally never heard anything from Mr. Trump or his kids that could be characterized as a lie. In a 2009 article entitled "Donald Trump's 6 Secrets to Keeping Your Edge in Life," the then 63-year-old listed as number two "Make Your Communications Short, Fast and Direct." He goes on to say, "In any conversation, I give myself an internal deadline. I say as much as I can in as few words as possible." Being concise, cutting to the chase, is often a good thing.

Leaders must know when being concise is appropriate, as often more lengthy conversation is required. In today's environment, where virtually everything is recorded, it is also crucial that communication be timely and accurate. During the presidential debates the candidates used statistics and other information to support their position or to undermine the opponent. The news media, in doing post-debate analysis, immediately conducted fact-checking to let the American people know which statements were true or false. Mr. Trump was fact-checked incessantly, perhaps because he made many general remarks or made statements that reporters felt were inaccurate or grandiose, something he is known to do. For example, one of his signature campaign issues was to repeal the Affordable Care Act. Trump said in the second debate with Ms. Clinton that "the premiums are going up 60, 70, 80 percent. Next year they're going to go up over 100 percent." Some of the media say that his misstatements are not honest mistakes, but are intentional. At a roundtable on immigration with elected officials from California on May 16, 2018, President Trump called MS-13 gang members "animals." The media went wild, accusing Trump of calling all immigrants animals, which was not the case. He was referring specifically to gang members who brutally kill people. The opposition party and the media that endorses it called Trump's remark intentional. Either way, President Trump's communication style gives ammunition to his detractors every single day.

Leaders must communicate effectively, openly, and in a timely fashion. With all of the technology at our fingertips, from I-phones to I-pads to Google and Facebook, how to do this best is an almost overwhelming task. Each company has a culture and an employee demographic (things like age and socio-economic status), and those things should be looked at when determining how best to communicate. I wonder if the personnel folks at the White House do anything to gauge the employees' attitudes, or if they conduct surveys, roundtables, and the like. They could start with an employee survey to learn how employees feel about the current state of communications. The results of the survey could provide the foundation for improvement. Often, employees have the best suggestions to increase the effectiveness of communications. The days of employee bulletin boards are gone – millennials want text messages and instant information. Other workers may prefer something to hold and read. It is necessary to ensure that upper management communicate with all groups in a company, which means transmitting information – including legal and insurance-related information and privacy notices. Here are some things to consider:

- What to communicate and how to get in front of a negative story

- What vehicles should be used (memos, emails, newsletter, meetings, notices, text messages, social media)

- How often to communicate

- How to target communications (for example, sending a message that the CEO is leaving versus announcing a new menu in the cafeteria)

- How internal messaging mirrors external communications

The bottom line is that employees want to be in the know. White House employees and those in the administration, many of whom had no previous political experience, likely may need more information. Obviously, some things are not communicated for security reasons. There are varying degrees of security clearance that depend largely on one's position in the government. Some personnel are entrusted with the most secure and confidential information. They must be properly vetted and receive the necessary clearances. In my opinion, Mr. Trump as president could do a better job in this area.

Former New Jersey Governor Chris Christie, who was part of Trump's campaign and one of the first Republicans to endorse him, said on his book tour that President Trump, early on, made some bad hires. Christie said of the people Trump appointed or hired that "far too often he's found himself saddled with the riffraff."[16] Christie cites those with no political experience like Rex Tillerson, who was appointed Secretary of State, while in contrast he believes Trump hasn't hired enough of folks like Steve Mnuchin or Kellyanne Conway.

When I worked for him, Trump hired some people based on his first impression or gut feeling. He has hired people in his administration who lacked the qualifications or experience needed for important jobs in government. Trump, in announcing any appointment, would tell the American people that the person was great, a good man or woman, highly competent – all adjectives that do not reveal experience. To be fair, in any business, some people are hired that may not be qualified, yet they become successful. In Trump's administration, some of the lesser qualified individuals were fired or resigned because they could not get the necessary clearances. In early 2019, Heather Nauert withdrew her name from consideration as the UN Ambassador to succeed Nikki Haley. At the time of her nomination, she was a communications spokesperson for the State Department, having been hired from Fox News. Heather's withdrawal letter stated that the previous few months had been a strain on her family. I believe that she may have realized that her lack of experience would lead to a failure to be confirmed after the Senate hearings. Either way, President Trump has said little and the communication on this topic has been quiet.

Perhaps the budget battle and seeking money for the wall, among other things, have taken precedence.

Chapter 4 Endnotes

[1] Tara Golshan, "Donald J. Trump's Strange Speaking Style," *Vox,* October 19, 2016.

[2] Michael Maslansky, "Communication Strategies from Donald Trump," *PR Daily,* January 28, 2016.

[3] Craig von Buseck, D.Min, "Why Reagan Was 'The Great Communicator'," www.cbn.com/.../perspectives/vonbuseck_reagan_tribute.aspx

[4] Ibid.

[5] Peggy Noonan, *Simply Speaking, How to Communicate your Ideas with Style,* (New York: Harper Collins, 1998).

[6] Craig von Buseck, same as #3 above

[7] Reagan's "Tear down that wall" speech

[8] https://en.wikipedia.org/wiki/Tear_down_this_wall

[9] Ibid.

[10] "Berlin Wall", *History.com Editors,* December 15, 2009. https://www.history.com/topics/cold-war/berlin-wall

[11] Jamie Dettmer, "Trump Proves That in Diplomacy, Body Language as Revealing as Words," *VOA News.com,* January 26, 2018.

[12] Matt Jones, "What Donald Trump's hand gestures really mean," *GQ Magazine,* June, 2017.

[13] Glenn Kessler, Salvador Rizzo and Meg Kelly, "Report: President Trump has made 3,001 false or misleading claims so far," *Washington Post,* May 1, 2018.

[14] Pamela Brown and Sarah Westwood, "Free-wheeling Mode of Operation," CNN, April 24, 2018.

[15] "How Martin Luther King Jr. Succeeded with Soft Skills,"

Conover, https://www.conovercompany.com/how-martin-luther-king-jr-succeeded-with-soft-skills/

[16] Chris Christie, *Let Me Finish: Trump, the Kushners, Bannon, New Jersey and the Power of In-Your-Face Politics* (New York: Hachette Books, 2019).

Chapter 5

Negotiating – The Art of the Deal
Win-Win – Learn Not Lose

Let us never negotiate out of fear. But let us never fear to negotiate

~ John F. Kennedy

Mr. Trump views his skills at negotiating as being at an extremely high level. He has acquired at least two of the properties in his vast empire by being, according to him, the better negotiator. In business and in life negotiation is vital and, for Trump, it is key to winning. His unpredictability, however, often confuses us when it comes to negotiation. We are seeing that up close and personal in his presidency.

I remember at Trump Hotel Collection when we put out RFPs (request for proposals) to various vendors for a back office system that would initially service two hotels, then additional properties. For anyone who has gone through this process, it is time-consuming, frustrating, and takes a lot of resources. We decided on our vendor of choice, but the price was out of our range. Mr. Trump assigned his son Eric to negotiate with the vendor. At the time, Eric was only in his early twenties, but he had learned from the master. After going back and forth, Eric basically told the vendor they could accept our final offer and use the Trump name in their testimonials, or we would go elsewhere. The vendor accepted the offer! I was pleasantly surprised at the negotiating skill Eric displayed at such a young age. It reminds me of a line in his father's Republican nomination acceptance speech, when Mr. Trump, speaking about the US trade agreements with China and others, said, "That includes negotiating NAFTA (North American Free Trade Agreement) to get a much better deal for America – and we'll walk away if we don't get the deal that we want."

Mr. Trump enjoys bragging that he uses the best appliances in his properties including Wolf, Sub-Zero, and Kohler. One day I heard the "Kohler story" from a long-time Trump employee. Mr. Kohler owns the famous American Club in Kohler, Wisconsin, plus two golf resorts, Blackwolf and Whistling

Straits, which are part of the company's hospitality division. More than 130 years ago, 29-year old John Kohler placed feet on a trough to create what we refer to today as the bathtub, which launched the Kohler brand. In the company's early days, the Kohlers, looking for workers, built dormitory-style residences complete with laundry facilities, dining halls, and whatever else was needed for the workers to live comfortably. It would be interesting to know about the negotiations that went on during that time to make this type of deal come to fruition. The Kohlers were able to provide work as well as room and board to immigrants from various countries. In 1981 the Kohlers refurbished the American Club into a five-star, five-diamond luxury resort with four golf courses, nine restaurants, and the Kohler water Spa. The Spa is just one of 47 in the United States rated five-star by Forbes. My former colleague told me that Mr. Kohler and Mr. Trump are longtime friends. They made a deal by which Trump purchases toilets from Kohler for the Trump properties and Mr. Trump can visit Mr. Kohler's luxury resort whenever he wishes. In the glossy, colorful brochure for Trump International Las Vegas, on "the perfect home" page is listed "lavish European style kitchens appointed with Wolf and Sub-Zero appliances." Bosch is mentioned on the pamphlet portion which describes the one-bedroom condominium. I'm guessing that Kohler is not mentioned only because most people probably are not looking at the manufacturer of their toilet. In any event Mr. Trump, who chooses the best, is impressed I'm sure by the fact that Kohler properties are recipients of the highest praise in the hotel industry.

In *The Art of the Deal*, Trump describes negotiating by saying, "My style of deal-making is quite simple and straight-forward. I aim very high, and then I just keep pushing and pushing to get what I'm after."[1] To some people, this may sound like a bully, and Trump has been called that in both business and politics. Either way, he has a drive to get what he wants. It has been tougher, no doubt, as president, since he has many more people to negotiate with than in a typical business undertaking. And what he wants and the other side wants are often diametrically opposed. I do believe, however, that part of the issue with some politicians on both sides is that they loathe President Trump and will not support anything he endorses. Additionally, it takes extremely effective negotiating to manage complex worldwide relationships, wars around the globe, and domestic conflicts. Trump told the world on the campaign trail that he could handle all of these things ... and more. What he may have failed to fully realize is the difference between negotiating a business deal and negotiating the resolution of a major conflict. In his business undertakings, a goal would be to determine how much money there was, the options to structure the deal and then to pen an agreement that provided the most financial value. In conflicts between nations, the negotiator must first break down the barriers that are preventing a solution in order to reach a deal. In *Think Like a Champion* Trump says, "Someone who analyzed my negotiating technique said I had an advantage over most people because I had the ability to get to the point faster than anybody else." He goes on to say that "there's a balance to successful negotiation ... the best negotiation is when both sides win." [2]

Not everyone agrees with President Trump about his self-professed acumen for negotiating. Bess Levin says "Any success Trump had in business occurred at the very beginning of his career."[3] She goes on to speak about Trump's book *The Art of the Deal,* written with ghostwriter Tony Schwartz.

Apparently, Schwartz has said that Mr. Trump basically just agreed to all of his demands, including "an almost unheard half of the $500,000 advance from Random House and also half of the royalties." Deepak Malhotra told Politico "What should have been a great deal on a book about negotiation actually is one of the most interesting pieces of evidence that he's not a good negotiator ... I don't think there's a better ghostwriting deal out there."[4]

At the World Economic Forum in Davos, Switzerland, on January 26, 2018, President Trump told the attendees, "The United States is prepared to negotiate mutually beneficial, bilateral trade agreements with all countries. This will include countries within The Trans-Pacific Partnership, which are very important. We have agreements with several of them already. We would consider negotiating with the rest either individually or perhaps as a group if it is in the interests of all." As time goes on in his presidency, I believe that President Trump will better understand the difference between negotiating on the world stage versus a business negotiation. We should be grateful that he has experienced key advisors leading the charge on many fronts, including Secretary of State Mike Pompeo.

During the North Atlantic Treaty Organization (NATO) Conference in Brussels in July, 2018, ahead of the Trump-Putin Summit, President Emmanuel Macron of France turned the tables on Trump. President Trump, it was reported, told Macron that he should persuade the European Union to negotiate with the United States, and Macron replied that he was not in favor of negotiating under threat. Macron apparently then said to Trump, "I read *The Art of the Deal*. I know that we need to retaliate first so we have some leverage in the negotiation."

Mr. Trump is known for his use of pre-conditions or

ultimatums when negotiating, for setting lofty goals for deal-making, and for a "we win they lose" mentality. On the campaign trail he consistently told crowds that he would negotiate the best trade deals for America. It sounded honest, feasible, and right to millions of voters. Trump often spoke of the Iran deal, signed under President Obama, by saying "It will go down in history as one of the worst deals ever negotiated." The Iran deal is supposed to prevent Iran from acquiring a nuclear weapon and the United States gave Iran, according to President Trump, $150 billion dollars to sign the agreement. Under the Obama administration, the Iranian side said we simply unfroze the $150 billion, as it was their money. Trump also said about the Iran deal: "We won't be using a man like Senator Kerry that has absolutely no concept of negotiation." Now the shoe is on the other foot, and we will see how it plays out. So far in his first term he has been unable to successfully negotiate a deal to repeal and replace the Affordable Care Act, which was a promise to the American people, and that he said would be done on day one of his presidency. And rather than take any responsibility for this, he blamed the other party. During the discussions over the first budget under President Trump, who had promised to get things done, Senate minority leader Chuck Schumer told reporters, "The parties were negotiating quite well until Donald Trump and the White House threw a monkey wrench into it." Nothing bipartisan here ... both sides just believe they are better negotiators. "President Trump tells people he keeps the world guessing with his wild unpredictability. But those who work most closely with him say he's a one-trick pony in negotiations."[5]

One thing I know for certain, having worked for Mr. Trump, is that his negotiation skills should be an asset in Washington,

D.C., at least insofar as financial matters are concerned. I believe many of his base voted for him because he was not a politician and they perceived he had financial acumen. In fact, even before he took office, he was making economic deals with big players like Boeing, which had received a contract with the Air Force for the new Air Force One jets. The anticipated cost at the time was around $4 billion. A month after the election, the president-elect tweeted that he wanted to cancel the order, saying Boeing was "doing a little bit of a number." The list price for two of the planes was around $757 million – the added cost included customization for presidential aircraft. Boeing's CEO Dennis Muilenburg met with President Trump in December, 2016 to outline options for lowering the cost, all of which were rejected by the Air Force. The president called for $1 billion in savings while Boeing is taking financial hits in overruns on the new KC-46A tanker. In September of 2017, the Air Force awarded a contract modification for just under $600 million for designs for the presidential aircraft, whereas they had originally quoted $4 billion before President Trump negotiated with Boeing.

The American public has heard for decades about the misuse of taxpayer money in Washington, the exorbitant costs that government agencies, including the Pentagon, are charged on items for which a business would pay a fraction. Everything government does (from administering Medicare to running the Veteran's Administration), has been shown to be more expensive than the private sector. So when candidate Trump promised to "drain the swamp," millions of Americans were on board with that. On October 18, 2016, during the final weeks of the campaign, when it looked like Ms. Clinton had the election in the bag, Trump introduced his "drain the swamp" five-point ethics plan concerning lobbyists. He wasn't interested in negotiating any aspects of the plan, because he had pledged to cut the bureaucracy and clean out the corruption in Washington, and lobbyists were part of the problem as he saw it. However, in the last few months of his campaign, he went through three high-level campaign surrogates who some accused of being part of the swamp – Paul Manafort, Corey Lewandowski, and David Bossie. Lewandowski and Bossie co-authored *"Let Trump Be Trump,"* and they received a lot of airtime, particularly on Fox News, while promoting the book. They then co-authored *"Trump's Enemies"* and are enjoying more financial success. Paul Manafort, the campaign chair, resigned on August 16, 2016, days after new campaign manager Kellyanne Conway and Steve Bannon of Breitbart News joined the Trump campaign.

Manafort had no choice but to leave, as he had been plagued by allegations about ties to the pro-Russian government in Ukraine and his involvement in business dealings between Russia and Ukraine. Manafort has an interesting past, and a long association with Mr. Trump. He built a career that spanned over three decades in Washington D.C., and worked on both the Ronald Reagan and George H.W. Bush presidential campaigns. He founded two lobbying firms, with clients including Ferdinand Marcos, the former dictator of the Philippines. After 2008, Manafort seemed to vanish from the Washington scene and his firm, Davis Manafort, was not much heard from.

With numerous international clients, Manafort became involved in advising a pro-Russian named Yanukovych who knew that Davis Manafort was doing work for Ukranian oligarch Rinat Akhmetov. Former Manafort associates say that

Manafort's earnings ran into seven figures over several years. Yanukovych won the election as president of Ukraine in 2010, and apparently retained Manafort as an adviser. Whatever may or may not have happened, Manafort was arrested, sent to jail and subsequently convicted in August, 2018, on eight counts of tax fraud. President Trump sent out several tweets in which he praised Manafort and called what happened to him part of the Russian collusion investigation "witch hunt." As president, Trump would be able to pardon Manafort – it will be interesting to see if his loyalty goes that deep as Manafort waits in prison.

In June of 2017, Mr. Trump fired his first campaign manager, Corey Lewandowski, who it was said needed to be more disciplined. Lewandowski's influence was waning in the final months of his job (which paid $20,000 per month), as allegations swirled about him inappropriately grabbing a reporter, who was simply trying to ask a question. She pressed charges and Lewandowski was charged with simple battery. But two weeks later the Palm Beach County prosecutor said he would not prosecute. A couple of weeks after that Lewandowski was in the spotlight again, as he was accused of man-handling a protester. On June 20, 2016, he split from the Trump campaign, which some claimed was a firing, but was described as "amicable" by Donald Trump Jr. Lewandowski received severance money and was quickly hired by CNN as a contributor; however, he had signed a non-disclosure, which basically prevented him from talking about Mr. Trump. After Trump won the Republican nomination, he often went on camera and praised Lewandowski's efforts. Lewandowski, in addition to being a contributor on cable news and profiting from his book, has a consulting company in Delaware. They are not registered as lobbyists.

Perhaps the biggest and most crucial negotiation of Trump's presidency is with North Korea. In June, 2018 an unprecedented summit took place in Singapore between North Korea's Kim Jung Un and President Trump. It seems strange that just months before the summit both leaders were trading jabs with one another, President Trump nicknaming Kim "Little Rocket Man." Trump stated upfront that denuclearization was the goal, and the United States would accept nothing less. Kim, it's been said, is willing to give up his nukes if the United States makes a pledge not to attack North Korea. Mike Pompeo met with Kim Jung Un in April, 2018, before the entire world knew of it. Things appeared to be going well, and officials on both sides were working out details for the summit. Then, in the last week of May, President Trump penned a letter to Kim Jung Un essentially calling off the summit, which had been scheduled for June 12. Apparently, he was not happy about what he deemed were inflammatory remarks about Vice-President Pence, including that Pence was a "political dummy."

Many in the news media thought President Trump's letter was groveling, in that he thanked the North Korean dictator several times, including for the release of American hostages. In the letter Trump says, "I felt a wonderful dialogue was building up between you and me...." He goes on to say, "If you change your mind having to do with this most important summit, please do not hesitate to call me or write." This sounds like a business meeting approach rather than an attempt to achieve a historic rapprochement with the Korean dictator. But, surprisingly, it appears to have worked, as within hours of receiving Trump's letter the North Koreans responded by saying they were willing to talk to the United States "at any time, at any format." Kim Kye Gwan, first minister of foreign affairs, said the North was "willing to give the U.S. time and opportunities." The media, however, was not as complimentary to President Trump about the summit, saying that few details were provided.

Within moments of actually meeting Chairman Kim face to face, Trump told the entire world on national television that the two men now had an "excellent relationship." After the brief one-on-one meeting, the two men signed a document which Trump said commits North Korea to working toward denuclearization. In return, President Trump stopped the joint military exercises with South Korea, characterizing them as "inappropriate" at that juncture. He did, however, say that sanctions would remain in place until the nukes are gone. Prior to the summit negotiation expert Marty Latz said, "Nothing may have a more direct impact on the safety, security, and prosperity of the world than Donald Trump's negotiation skills."[6]

Trump proclaimed that the world is safe and the North Korea threat gone, even without a timetable from North Korea. In response, Retired Army General Barry McCaffrey told NBC News, "First of all you've got to be honest with yourself. For the president to come home and say 'the nuclear threat from North Korea is gone, you can sleep safely at night,' is an element of fantasy. So, you have to be realistic – achievable, negotiating goals and deals with them from a position of strength and maintain your allies. We're doing none of that."

This is classic Trump; he is consistent in this regard. He reacts to something instantaneously rather than mulling things over and developing a strategy. And, for better or worse, it seems to be working for him. We know, based on his own words about being a candidate for the Nobel Peace Prize as a result of the historic summit, that he wanted it to happen more than anyone else did. He believes this would solidify his place in history and, if successful with denuclearization, would make him one of the greatest American presidents. We may never know what occurred behind the scenes when Mike Pompeo met with Kim Jong Un – the back and forth that took place and what if anything was truly achieved. One thing is certain, if denuclearization results from the talks with Kim, the entire world will hear about it from President Trump. Trump critics believed that he gave up too much too soon, with no timeline from North Korea on denuclearization. It is an interesting time in his presidency and in the world. In successful negotiations, both sides give something to get something, plain and simple.

A second summit was held in early 2019 and the President had high expectations and hopes for a deal. When it appeared that it would not conclude with a signed treaty, the summit was cut short and all parties went home. Complicating matters is the fact that Kim Jung Un has since met with Vladimir Putin as the world waits and wonders.

Perhaps one of the most significant successful negotiations in our nation's history was over the Cuban Missile Crisis, sometimes referred to as the Thirteen Days in October. In October 1962 the world was on the brink of nuclear war after an American spy plane secretly photographed Soviet missile sites on the island of Cuba. The Soviet Union put the missiles in Cuba to support Fidel Castro, who had overthrown the American-backed dictator, Fulgencio Batista, in 1959. Castro declared in 1961 that Cuba had joined the Soviet Bloc, and that is why the Soviets placed the missiles there – to protect their ally. Cuba is less than 100 miles from south Florida. All schools at the time simulated drills so that everyone inside the buildings would know how to prepare for an attack. I vividly remember being instructed by the nuns that when the alarm sounded we were to take cover under our desks and place our hands over our ears. It was a frightening time for everyone, as the world waited and hoped for a peaceful end to the crisis.

Many secret meetings had been held within the Kennedy administration before the press and the American people knew what was going on. Kennedy first met secretly with his advisers, as he did not want Cuba or the Soviet Union to know of the discovery of the missiles. The president learned of the missiles on October 16 and subsequently met with Bobby Kennedy, his attorney general, and other advisers. The president signed a National Security Action Memorandum to formally establish the Executive Committee to the National Security Council (EXCOMM), with the first meeting taking place on October 23.

The three options that the EXCOMM came up with regarding how to handle the crisis were: 1) an airstrike without warning; 2) a blockade (later referred to as a quarantine); and 3) an airstrike to take out the missiles followed by an invasion of Cuba. The blockade was not endorsed by Vice President Lyndon Johnson, and the airstrike was likened to what the Japanese had done to us at Pearl Harbor. Ultimately, the decision was to go with the blockade, which began on Sunday, October 22.

Kennedy placed a naval blockade around Cuba, which would prevent the Soviets from bringing in additional military supplies. In the days that followed, Prime Minister Nikita Khrushchev and the president exchanged letters in which both acknowledged that war had to be prevented. Khrushchev told Kennedy that the Soviets placed the missiles in Cuba for defensive purposes because Cuba could not be lost to China, the second largest communist country. In one of his letters, Khrushchev called for negotiation with the United States, as Kennedy had said he would take action if the missiles were not removed. Robert F. Kennedy, the president's brother and closest adviser, is largely credited with facilitation of the backdoor negotiations that ensued and ultimately put an end to the escalating crisis.

The negotiations included a 25-year secret deal brokered by Robert F. Kennedy and the Soviet ambassador Anatoly Dobrynin, under which the US agreed to remove its nuclear missiles from Turkey. The US also agreed to respect Cuba's sovereignty, not to invade the island or interfere in Cuba's government. Fifty years after the crisis was averted, in 2012, Nikita Khrushchev's son Sergei said, "The Cuban Missile Crisis showed that two leaders decided not to shoot first, but to think and negotiate with each other … negotiation was one of the biggest achievements of the Cuban Missile Crisis … the great lesson to come out of this is that you have to negotiate with your enemy…."[7]

Many books including those by Nikita Khrushchev, Robert F. Kennedy, and Robert McNamara, the secretary of defense at the time, as well as a movie, have been produced about the Cuban Missile Crisis. Each one details various accounts of the thirteen days. The American authors give credit to both Kennedys regarding the negotiation's success and proclaimed it a victory for the Kennedy presidency. Those thirteen days involved much time, effort, deliberation, determination, and compromise. Each side knew the stakes if the negotiations failed and the peril that could ensue.

During my career, my best negotiation was with the

various labor unions that I dealt with. Typically, negotiations start with the union presenting their proposal, including everything that they would like to achieve for the employees they represent. Meetings are conducted at which both sides talk about each proposal, and often every word in the proposal. To say that these meetings can be laborious (no pun intended), is an understatement. It is not unusual, particularly for a first contract, that negotiations take a minimum of one year. Negotiations also take place when employees file grievances and the employer and the union take various steps to try to resolve them. In my experience, successful union negotiations start with relationships. Each party must respect the other, listen to their views, and work toward a goal that is good for the employee and satisfies union demands. I remember my first role as director of human resources in a hotel that was unionized shortly after opening. My philosophy with the union was simple: we, the employer, wanted good employees and the union should want good members. And during my tenure there, that is what we worked to achieve. Something else that should be mentioned is that the employer is not always right. A grievance that has merit should be acknowledged and settled promptly. It is in everyone's best interest and, if it was the result of a mistake on the employer's part, admitting that goes a long way with employees.

When I was a new employee with the Trump Organization, Mr. Trump was regarded as a friend to the labor unions in New York. He hosted annual Christmas parties and invited labor leaders and union workers, including New York City police officers. Then, as now, he had a special affinity for the men and women in blue. During the holidays it was all about frivolity and relationships. I never heard him or his kids say anything negative about the unions. In fact, I believe he understood that labor peace was essential in business. Fighting with the unions, spending countless hours and a lot of money trying to settle an otherwise petty grievance, was not the norm. He worked with and around unions in New York for decades. In Las Vegas, both before the hotel opened and during my tenure, we were nonunion. It was the employees' choice. At the time, our hourly rates were among the highest in the city, our benefits were competitive, and the working environment was good. I have no personal knowledge of what happened during the years after I left, although I did read all of the reports and stories regarding the Hotel Employees and Restaurant Employees (H.E.R.E.) Local 226 campaign to unionize the the Trump property.

When Eric Trump visited Las Vegas during the presidential campaign, he was quoted in the media as saying it was not management's decision to be union or not; rather, it was the decision of the employees through a vote. Ultimately, the H.E.R.E. union asked for an election, the Trump employees voted and the union won the election. During Mr. Trump's presidential campaign and on his visits to Las Vegas, there was picketing at his hotel and at or near his speech locations, one of which was Treasure Island on the Las Vegas strip. The hotel is owned by his Trump Las Vegas partner, Phil Ruffin, and the workers are represented by H.E.R.E. Local 226. It is a common tactic used by the unions and not specifically targeted at the Trump organization.

Certainly, neither President Trump nor his sons are negotiating labor contracts – that is left up to local-level executives. I am certain everyone wants what is best for the employees, as it is good for business and good for the customer. It is a winning strategy and one that can be achieved through negotiation. Each side must know at the outset what they are willing to compromise on and what they will not accept. The recent long government shutdown was a negotiation tactic utilized by President Trump. He held out until the Democrat majority in the House was able to push him in a corner. For political, economic, and humanitarian reasons, the shutdown finally ended and both sides claimed victory. In the end, the president used his trump card and declared a national emergency at the border to enable him to divert money to building the wall. Within a day, lawsuits were filed and Trump said he imagines this will go all the way up to the Supreme Court.

Negotiating is a learned and difficult skill to master. From parenting to relationships to work and everything in between, we are negotiating throughout our lives. Here are some things that can make negotiating easier and more successful.

- Education is the basis for all negotiations. You must learn about the other person or parties first, before anything. It is essential to know everything you can and to build rapport. It would be difficult to walk into a room, sit down, and immediately negotiate something without this critical first step.

- Preparation is key. Whether you are trying to negotiate with a spouse over which restaurant to go to or getting ready to negotiate the price of a car, you need to do your homework.

- Find out what it is the other person needs or wants.

For example, if you know someone is vegetarian, you wouldn't recommend a restaurant that has only non-vegetarian items on the menu.

- After these critical steps, first seek to understand the other person's point of view or logic. Ask for their rationale on whatever it is you are discussing.

- Documentation can be crucial in a negotiation. Often someone will make a claim that you may question or know not to be the case. Politely ask what documentation they can provide to validate their claim or position.

- Persuasion is a negotiation technique and it takes much effort and work. In order to influence others, whether in a political election or a union negotiation, there has to be a benefit to both sides. Until you build rapport, know the other side's logic and rationale, persuading would be difficult. Articulate a benefit that will give the other side what they need or want, or they will not be persuaded by what you say. Think win-win and begin with the end in mind.

Chapter 5 Endnotes

[1] Donald J. Trump with Tony Schwartz, *The Art of the Deal,* (New York: Random House, 1987).

[2] Donald J. Trump, *Think Like a Champion* (New York: Vanguard Press, 2009).

[3] Hive, "Donald Trump Has Always Been a Terrible Negotiator," Bess Levin, June 1, 2018.

[4] Politico, "He Pretty Much Gave In to Whatever They Asked For," Michael Kruse, June 1, 2018.

[5] The Atlantic, "Trump Almost Always Folds," David A. Graham, May 23, 2018.

[6] EA Worldview, "Trump Watch, 454: Trump Gives Himself an Exit from Meeting With North Korea's Kim," posted by Scott Lucas, Apr 19, 2018.

[7] "The Cuban Missile Crisis, 50 Years Later," https://news.brown.edu/articles/2012/10/missile

Chapter 6

Loyalty – Allegiance, Duty, Fidelity to Others
Family, Faith, Country

Loyalty is a way to recognize and reaffirm allegiance
~ Donald J. Trump

Much has been said and written about Mr. Trump's loyalty to his employees, friends, and family. In *The Art of the Deal* Trump says, "I'm loyal to people who've done good work for me." While I worked with those to whom Trump was loyal, his loyalty can also shift when he deems it appropriate. Trump has hired, fired, and rehired more people than any other person with whom I have worked. The White House during Trump's presidency has experienced more staff turnover than at any other time in its history, and many of the people who have left were dismissed by President Trump. The author Michael Kruse tells of conversations with people who like me have worked for Mr. Trump, and with those whom he has fired. Kruse writes, "He is both impulsive and intuitive, for better and for worse. He hires on gut instinct rather than qualifications ... he's loyal 'like, this great loyalty freak' as he once put it – except when he's not."[1] Barbara Res, who worked on and off for Trump for almost two decades on building projects in New York, notes that Fred Trump "taught Donald that honest employees were stupid, and anyone with any brains would steal his boss blind. So, Donald turned to his family for their loyalty."[2]

Mr. Trump's former longtime attorney and confidant, in the past sometimes referred to as his sixth child, is Michael Cohen. Mr. Cohen revealed his loyalty to Trump in an interview with *Vanity Fair*. Cohen said, "There are guys who are very loyal to him that would have gone in (to the White House), but there was a concerted effort by high-ranking individuals to keep out loyalists."[3] He goes on to say, "I'm the guy who would take a bullet for the President...."[4] Toward the end of the interview, Cohen tells the reporter he thinks that President Trump will be loyal to him, should he need him to be. After President Trump several times denied allegations of sexual misconduct, Cohen admitted to paying $130,000 of his own money to a porn star. Cohen originally said President Trump was not aware of the payment. Common Cause, a watchdog group, sent a letter to Rod Rosenstein, Deputy Attorney General, on January 22, 2018, with a complaint that the money paid in October 2016 to the porn star was legally questionable. The payment to Ms. Stephanie Clifford (better known as Stormy Daniels), may have violated reporting requirements and contribution limits under the Federal Election Campaign Act. Ms. Clifford was paid to keep silent about her alleged extramarital affair with Mr. Trump, which she says occurred in 2005.

President Trump has categorically denied the affair and any knowledge about a payment to the woman; however, Cohen has produced an audio tape which says otherwise. President Trump tweeted, "Inconceivable that the government would break into a lawyer's office (early in the morning) – almost unheard of ... even more inconceivable that a lawyer would tape a client – totally unheard of & perhaps illegal. The good news is that your favorite President did nothing wrong." Before Michael Cohen was indicted, Trump said on Twitter that Cohen would be loyal to him, tweeting, "Michael, a fine person with a wonderful family. Michael is a businessman for his own account/lawyer who I always liked & respected." Trump then turned around and said on Twitter in July, 2018 that "this one-time ally has now turned foe ... what kind of a lawyer would tape a client ... so sad! Is this a first, never heard of it before...." It is quite interesting since that tweet how things have developed – that now both men loathe one another. Cohen pleaded guilty, has testified in secret and in public before Congress, and is now serving time in prison for his crimes.

I saw Mr. Trump promote individuals based on their

loyalty into positions they likely would never have attained in any other organization. That was his way of operating in business, and now we have seen it carry over into the White House. The second general manager at the Trump Hotel in Las Vegas started out as Mr. Trump's bodyguard. He then received a promotion, moved to Las Vegas and was put in charge of the construction project during the building of the hotel. After the property opened, he moved into an office in the hotel and continued on the payroll. He often spoke with Mr. Trump and his family, and personally escorted them to wherever they went when they visited Las Vegas. At the start of the recession in 2008, after we had changed some things and laid off employees, our first general manager left, and Mr. Trump promoted the construction manager and former bodyguard into the position. I like to think he is successful in part because he had a great team around him, and we taught him what he needed to know. It pleases me when people get their chance, and this individual certainly did, based on his loyalty to Mr. Trump. On the campaign trail, Trump the candidate said about loyalty, "Folks, look, I'm a loyal person. I'm going to be loyal to the country." He went on to say, "It's so important, and it's one of the traits that I most respect in people. You don't see it enough, you don't see it enough ... and it's a two-way street. I really expect them to be loyal to me." The article mentions my former general manager, described above, and states that he has said of his promotions within the Trump Organization, "I probably wouldn't have been able to do that anywhere else."[5]

The Trump administration started out as a group of loyalists (Steve Bannon, Jared Kushner, Jeff Sessions, Hope Hicks). These people would never, in my humble opinion, have gotten their positions except in a Trump administration.

Some who have worked for him say that Trump can ensure total loyalty by hiring people based on his patronage. In the White House, where government rules and hiring practices are much different than in the Trump Organization (where Mr. Trump could just say, "you're hired"), demanding loyalty has raised eyebrows. Along the way, the world is watching and speculating about the tumult as numerous loyalists have fallen by the wayside (Spicer, Priebus, Bannon, Gorka, Scaramucci). Others whom the president himself appointed, have either fallen from grace or just had too much of the shenanigans and either resigned or were asked to leave (H.R. McMaster, the national security advisor, Rex Tillerson, secretary of state, Gary Cohn, director of the national economic council).

Omarosa Marigault-Newman, former director of communications for the Office of Public Liaison, who was fired three times by Trump during the *Apprentice* runs, said she resigned, although initial reports had us believing she created a commotion after a meeting with John Kelly and was escorted from the White House. Her version of what happened, as well as her admission of taping conversations with Ivanka Trump, her husband Jared Kushner, and with General Kelly in the situation room are included in her book, *Unhinged: An Insider Account of the Trump White House*. She had her interviews on many of the networks and exposed disturbing details including taping conversations in the White House, but since then little has been heard from her.

The one holdover from the Obama Administration, Secretary of Veteran Affairs David Shulkin, resigned after numerous ethics violations came to light. Shulkin described the Washington environment as "toxic, chaotic, disrespectful, and subversive." The truth of the turnover matter is that within approximately one year at least a dozen high-level appointees have either resigned or been fired. On March 13, 2018, John McEntee lost his security clearance as a result of an investigation into his personal finances. McEntee was subsequently hired as a senior adviser to the Trump re-election campaign. Again, an example of how Trump can fire someone and then rehire the person in a different capacity.

All companies and every administration have personnel changes, particularly early on in a transition. Unfortunately, with the Trump administration the numbers are high and some of the departures have come as the result of shady practices, ethics concerns, and tumult. I'm sure the president is aware that leaders should praise in public and criticize in private, but it is his style to tell the world exactly what he is thinking and to put it in a tweet, without taking a moment to think about the consequences. The Environmental Protection Agency's head, Scott Pruitt, finally tendered his resignation to President Trump and despite months of alleged ethics violations, Trump continued to support Pruitt and extol his performance as head of the agency. Pruitt, who was confronted by protesters telling him to resign while he was eating dinner in a D.C. restaurant, told Trump in his lengthy resignation letter that the attacks on him and his family had taken a toll. I think the agency and the administration suffered a bigger toll, Mr. Pruitt.

Many folks associated with Trump the businessman or Trump the president end up crashing and burning. Sean Spicer, the first press secretary, came into the role with stellar credentials; however, from the get-go he sparred with the press and did not seem to have the demeanor appropriate for the position. Others with impressive careers end up imploding or getting caught up in something they were ill-prepared for.

Anthony Scaramucci, a wealthy businessman who stumped for Trump in the early days of the campaign, was selected by Trump as his third director of communications. He came off as boisterous and aggressive, and let it be known that he intended to make a lot of changes. Unfortunately for him, he went on a rant that was subsequently publicized and after less than two weeks on the job he heard the famous words, "you're fired." Scaramucci has since been on numerous Fox News shows, and also pops up on other networks, including CNN, to add his commentary about all things Trump. In a case like his, the firing has likely brought him more publicity than if he had stayed in the administration. He published *Trump: Blue Collar President* in late October, 2018.

Tony Schwartz, the ghostwriter on *The Art of the Deal,* said of Trump, "People are not people to him, they are instruments of his ego. And, when they serve his ego, they survive, and when they don't, they pass into the night."[6]

Chris Christie, a friend of Trump's long before the 2016 campaign, says of Trump, "He commands extraordinary loyalty from his supporters".[7] Christie gave his unflinching support and loyalty to Trump once he dropped out of the 2016 presidential race. Christie campaigned for Trump and after the election victory became part of the transition team. Christie said after the election that the only job he was interested in was attorney general. Unfortunately for him, President Trump nominated Jeff Sessions for the post. Sessions was doomed from the start as he recused himself from the Russian collusion investigation, and Trump ridiculed and bashed him incessantly after that. Things seemed to be going well for Christie until the day after the election when he was called to the White House and banished by Steve Bannon. According to Christie, who was going to blow the lid off of the decision that day with reporters, Bannon dangled the carrot of attorney general in front of him as they spoke, so the meeting continued for quite some time. By now everyone knows that Governor Christie prosecuted Jared Kushner's father, who subsequently went to prison. Kushner never forgot, and it was reported that he was the one who decided there was no place in the administration for Christie.

On March 29, 2017, President Trump signed an executive order establishing the Commission on Combating Drug Addiction and the Opioid Crisis, which he announced on national television. He named Chris Christie as the chairperson, saying he and the members would work closely with the White House Office of American Innovation (led by Jared Kushner!). The commission met five times during 2017, and issued a final report to the president before it disbanded. I wonder if Christie hoped, after chairing this commission, if a more permanent job in the administration was waiting for him. Until his book was published in early 2019, he had remained silent on the issue. Now the shoe is on the other foot and the real story, according to Christie, is coming out.

Much has occurred since the Cohen saga began, including James Comey's book, *A Higher Loyalty*. He started his media tour, including television interviews, in order to among other things clear his name and set the record straight. Comey said he never wanted to write a memoir and that his book is not one; rather, it's a book about leadership. In his first interview, with ABC the day before the book's release, Comey revealed several things. Interestingly, he thinks the meeting he had with President Trump in which Trump asked him to halt the FBI investigation of Michael Flynn, the former national security adviser, constitutes obstruction of justice. Second, he says Trump's firing of him was a "crazy" move, as he was leading the investigation of Russian influence in the 2016 election. Third, Comey said that firing Special Counsel Robert Mueller would be "the most serious attack yet on the rule of law." Comey also does not rule out that the Russians may have compromising information on the president. Fourth, Comey stands by his handling of the Hillary Clinton email server investigation. In fact, he intimates that he believed she was going to be elected, so re-opening the case was the right thing to do. If she had gotten elected, people would say that it was not fair and square! Finally, and coming from Comey this is not shocking, he calls President Trump "morally unfit" to be president. He cites examples such as how Trump handled the Charlottesville situation, how he talks about and treats women, and the constant lies, big and small, that Trump tells the American people. Additionally, and this also is not surprising, Comey said that President Trump is "untethered to truth" and "ego-driven."

Prior to the allegations of Russian collusion in the 2016 election, the most notorious political scandal in recent history involved President Richard Nixon in 1972. The events that transpired were bad enough, but the cover-up by the president led to his resignation, which was a first for our democracy. A break-in by five men at the Democratic National Committee (DNC) headquarters in the Watergate complex in Washington, D.C., led to arrests, convictions, and imprisonment for several people. Once caught (during their second burglary attempt), much of the evidence was turned over to John Dean, White House counsel to the President. While still employed as Nixon's attorney, Dean asked the president for immunity from prosecution for any crimes committed; however, the president refused. Nixon fired John Dean on the same day he accepted resignations from two other advisers involved in the scandal. Dean pleaded guilty to obstruction of justice, including payments of hush money to the burglars. Dean was sentenced to one to four years and his attorney successfully negotiated a reduced sentence. He ended up serving four months and was disbarred.

Like Mr. Cohen, Dean hired an attorney and started cooperating with the Senate committee investigating the scandal. With Dean's cooperation it became clear that there was a cover-up by Nixon, who had secretly recorded many of their meetings. "The term 'Watergate,' by metonymy, has come to encompass an array of clandestine and often illegal activities undertaken by members of the Nixon administration."[8] John Dean has said about Michael Cohen, "There are several parallels between my testimony ... and Michael Cohen's testimony about President Trump and his business practices."[9] He goes on to say that:

> Mr. Cohen should understand that if Mr. Trump is removed from office, or defeated in 2020, in part because of his testimony, he will be reminded of that for the rest of his life. He will be blamed by Republicans but appreciated by Democrats. If he achieves anything short of discovering the cure for cancer, he will always live in this pigeonhole. How did I know this? I am still dealing with it.[10]

Dean went on to become an author and lecturer speaking about his White House days, and wrote two books focused on Watergate. He is in the process of revising his 2006 book, *Conservatives Without Conscience,* to include his take on President Trump and his followers. Like Cohen, he was loyal to his boss, the president, until he was in his own personal crisis and was left to fend for himself.

Years ago, American workers were loyal to their companies, and many of them spent an entire career with one company. The corporate world and the workforce have both changed. In my experience, there is little loyalty to a company and more loyalty to a boss. At the Trump Organization, for example, we were successful in recruiting many of the people we worked with, based on prior associations. I brought dozens of people to Trump – people whom I had worked with two or even three times in the past. I have found in my career that if individuals respect and like someone, and workers and leaders are loyal to one another, people will follow that person. Time and again Mr. Trump has promoted people in the Trump Hotel Collection based on their performance; on their doing good work and being loyal. This was the case with the manager of the Washington, D.C. property, who had formerly been the general manager of Trump Toronto. He started his Trump career as the director of finance at Trump Chicago. I worked with him on both the Chicago and Toronto openings. Mr. Trump liked his look and his financial acumen. People who have good numbers skills, high intelligence quotients, and good test scores all are viewed positively by President Trump, and he has said so during his rally speeches. This GM did good work for Mr. Trump, and Mr. Trump rewarded him by placing him on the biggest stage at the Trump International Hotel in Washington, D.C. The Hotel has received unprecedented accolades, and is the only five-star property in the city.

Hope Hicks is another example of loyalty to Trump, both in the White House and before she joined the administration. She was a 29-year-old college graduate with some public relations experience who had the appearance, confidence, and polish that Trump loves. After a short tenure at Hiltzik Strategies, a public relations firm whose clients included Ivanka Trump and Jared Kushner companies, she went to work for Ivanka Trump. Hope caught Mr. Trump's eye and he placed her on the campaign trail. Officially, she was the campaign's spokesperson, although I do not remember ever hearing her speak. I've read that she was not comfortable doing so. After Trump was elected, so the story goes, Trump told her that she was going to work for him in the White House. Her title was White House communications director, and the media reported that she was very much behind the scenes; she was not on social media and did not do interviews. Rather, she was the gatekeeper for President Trump, deciding when he would do interviews, and with whom. As with Trump the businessman, he has people around him who do nothing but print articles, review tweets, and google his name so that he can see what is being written and said about him. When there is anything negative, he hits back, typically on Twitter.

If a reporter says something unfavorable about him, that person is banned for a period of time. CNN reported that there was major turmoil in the White House concerning Hicks dating Rob Porter, who resigned amid allegations of domestic violence made by two ex-wives. A day after Ms. Hicks testified behind closed doors to an investigative body, she announced her resignation. Sources close to Hicks said that she was contemplating leaving Washington, D.C., as she had spent three years there. She went back to Connecticut to pursue other opportunities. Hope was sighted getting on Air Force One during one of President Trumps' summer trips to Bedminster, New Jersey. There were rumors that she would either rejoin the administration or the 2020 campaign. Hicks has since been hired by Fox News as their senior communications person. Everything I've read about her and her time in the administration is so stellar that one wonders how a 29-year-old with virtually no experience could be that impressive to President Trump. While several communication directors who preceded Hicks left the job without words of praise from the president, that was not the case with Hope. In fact, President Trump tweeted "Hope is outstanding and has done great work for the last three years. She is as smart and thoughtful as they come, a truly great person. I will miss having her by my side but when she approached me about pursuing other opportunities, I totally understood. I am sure we will work together again in the future."

Back to the issue of loyalty. It is a quality that does not develop overnight. Workers are loyal to a boss or a company after they are typically the recipients of behavior befitting a boss who is himself loyal. Someone who has done good work is not necessarily loyal. Some reporters/journalists say the Hope Hicks resignation announcement a day after her testimony, wherein she admitted to "telling white lies" on behalf of the president, was a coincidence. It was also reported that President Trump was not at all happy about her white lies comment. And we know what happens when the president isn't happy... the tweets fly, he gets agitated, and people start falling by the wayside. In any case, few staffers are left from the Trump campaign. Some say the chaos in the administration is so toxic that soon only Trump himself may be left there.

Others opine that it's difficult to find personnel to work for Trump and those who do, when they depart, have trouble getting good jobs. Personally, I doubt that that is true – look at all the folks who have left and, it seems within days, are paid contributors on a major network, or they start their own radio show or a new company. I don't think any of them are going into the unemployment lines.

It's been widely reported that Trump is on record saying loyalty is the number one value he cherishes in an employee. Perhaps that is why he asked FBI Director James Comey for his loyalty (according to Comey). Comey talked about a private dinner he had with President Trump at the White House on January 27, 2017, during which the president repeatedly asked him for a pledge of loyalty. Comey maintains that President Trump said, "I need loyalty, I expect loyalty." Comey answered by saying, "You will always get honesty from me." Comey says the president then said, "That is what I want, honest loyalty." Trump has repeatedly denied he asked for a pledge of loyalty and says furthermore that he will testify to that. In fact, Trump has said that the question of loyalty never came up. Sarah Sanders, when asked at a White House news briefing if loyalty was a factor in selecting a new FBI Director said that Trump wants someone who is "loyal to the justice system."

Trump sees everyone in the administration as his employee, and it is natural for a boss to expect loyalty. Here is yet another example of how Trump the businessman tries to bring that mindset to Washington. Loyalty to America, the flag, the institution of the presidency is what a president should expect. Asking for loyalty to Trump personally takes on an entirely different meaning, including possibly being asked to do things one should not do. Government appointees swear an oath to "support and defend the Constitution of the United States against all enemies, foreign and domestic."

On the FBI's website there is an essay about the significance of the oath of office. FBI Academy legal instructor Jonathan Rudd writes "that we take an oath to support and defend the Constitution and not an individual leader, ruler, office or entity... a government based on individuals – who are inconsistent, fallible and often prone to error – too easily leads to tyranny on the one extreme or anarchy on the other."

When asked on Tucker Carlson's Fox News show about the Comey pledge of loyalty, former campaign manager Corey Lewandowski said, "Look, what the President asked for was loyalty to the country and loyalty to make sure the American people have the justice system that they want." This hardly seems likely, given that government appointees already take an oath of loyalty to the country. In this regard Lewandowski is maintaining his loyalty to President Trump.

Even people who started out loyal to President Trump have been humiliated and abandoned by him. Rex Tillerson, the former secretary of state, learned he was fired in a tweet from the president. It was known for some time that they had differences of opinion, but it seems that after Tillerson called Trump a "moron," things went downhill rapidly. So one has to ask who would, after seeing people destroyed, humiliated, and hung out to dry, want to work for this administration and take an oath of loyalty to the president. Attorney General Jeff Sessions rightly recused himself from the Russia investigation, but the president never forgot it and it led to Sessions' early departure.

Trump the president needs to understand that ethics and honesty trump loyalty. Anything else amounts to incompetence and corruption, and this White House has had scandals relating to both. The premium that President Trump places on loyalty has reshaped his original cabinet, and he is filling posts with either those who lack integrity, or is destroying the integrity of those loyalists he appoints. Either way, it is not befitting of the office of the presidency. Trump has consistently shown that he is loyal to himself and his family. He has switched political affiliations over the decades, typically choosing to go with whoever is in power, not unlike Winston Churchill. Despite his loathing of China's trade practices, Trump continues to make goods there and supported his daughter's line of merchandise, much of it made in China. Some may ask: Where is the presidents' loyalty to the American people?

Perhaps the most devoted surrogate has been Vice President Mike Pence. He is loyal to a fault, always praising the president when he (Pence) is in front of a microphone, regardless of the topic. Pence knows his place and it is being subservient to the president. Pence, after all, is an experienced politician. Jill Martin, VP and assistant general counsel for the Trump Organization, when asked during the campaign what Trump wants in a VP, said "Many of the same qualities that he would look for someone to work closely with him within his organization are going to apply to his search for a VP." We know that loyalty is at the top of his list._

Studies have shown that employees are loyal to their supervisors and managers rather than to the company. When employees who are loyal get loyalty in return, they tend to become more vested in their company and to align their professional goals with the goals of the company. I have been loyal to many people over the years, having hired them two or three times at different companies where I was employed.

Often, when I left a company, those individuals would leave to go to a place where they could work with a supervisor or manager they knew. So how do leaders build loyalty? When discussing loyalty as a core value, think about these questions.

- Why is loyalty in relationships important?

- What does loyalty feel like to you, in a relationship?

- How is loyalty in business similar or different?

- What does it take for you to be loyal to your school, company, volunteer organization?

- How do you feel when someone is disloyal to you?

- What can a company do to show loyalty to employees?

Chapter 6 Endnotes

[1] Michael Kruse, "The Executive Mr. Trump," *Politico Magazine,* July/August 2016.

[2] Barbara Res, "Trump Isn't Crazy: He's Trump," *New York Times,* January 16, 2018.

[3] Emily Jane Fox, "Why am I Going to Continue to Be Silent?" *Vanity Fair,* July 23, 2018.

[4] Emily Jane Fox, "Michael Cohen Would Take a Bullet for Donald Trump," *Hive,* September 6, 2017.

[5] Jill Colvin, "Trump Touts Loyalty in Defending Campaign Manager," *AP News,* April 2016.

[6] Peter Baker and Maggie Haberman, "For Many, Life in Trump's Orbit Ends in a Crash Landing," *New York Times,* April 26, 2018.

[7] Chris Christie, *Let Me Finish: Trump, the Kushners, Bannon, New Jersey and the Power of In-Your-Face Politics,* (New York: Hachette Books, 2019).

[8] John Dean, *Wikipedia, The Free Encyclopedia.*

[9] John W. Dean, "John Dean: I Testified Against Nixon. Here's My Advice for Michael Cohen," *The New York Times,* March 1, 2019.

[10] Ibid.

Chapter 7

Think Big – People, Money and Effort
Go Lean – Big Things Come in Small Packages

Think big – you have to think anyway,
so why not think big?
~ Donald Trump

Thinking big involves being positive, dreaming, setting lofty goals, and believing in yourself. Mr. Trump did all of these things in his former life, and he continues to do so as president. Everything Donald J. Trump did as a businessman, he did big. For example, when he launched *The Apprentice* reality television show, he chose to sit in a big boardroom. He had a big private jet (a Citation X described by Trump as "the fastest private plane ever made") and a big city apartment of three stories and 30,000 square feet in Trump Tower. His book, *Think Like a Champion,* was given to all attendees at the first Trump Hotel Collection Leadership conference in New York, each copy inscribed with Mr. Trump's big signature. When announcing the building of Trump International Hotel and Tower Chicago in 2001, Trump said the skyscraper would be the tallest building in the world. After the events of 9/11, the building was scaled back and the design was revised several times. Big to Trump equates to greatest, the best.

Mickael Damelincourt was hired as the director of finance at the Trump Hotel Chicago during construction. He is from France and came to America as a college student, learning English while working in hotels. We partnered on combined corporate hotel projects, including developing and putting in place an employee benefits plan for the Chicago and Las Vegas properties. Mickael did an outstanding job in his role, and several years later Mr. Trump promoted him to general manager for the new Trump International Toronto. Mickael was tapped for his business acumen, experience, and loyalty to Mr. Trump. He was a logical choice for yet another step up, and became the managing director for Trump International Hotel in Washington, D.C. I see him hobnobbing with celebrities and journalists who have written books about Trump, as well as with diplomats and the president and his family. I recently caught up with Mickael when he was at the Bellagio in Las Vegas for a conference. He told me that he loves being in Washington, D.C., and that he is grateful to have been a Trump employee for more than ten years. Mickael is another example of a young person who came to this country to learn, graduated from college, worked hard and is now a hotelier extraordinaire. He and his team earned the prestigious Forbes Five Star Award in both 2018 and 2019, the only Five Star recipient in Washington, D.C. I've told Mickael that he has come a long way in twenty years.

In his campaign speeches and rallies Trump spoke of things that are "big league," including what he would do as president in his first hundred days. In his speech accepting the Republican nomination he spoke of his big plans to "Make America Great Again" (safety at home, secure borders, adding millions of jobs to the economy, liberate our citizens from the crime and terrorism and lawlessness that threatens their communities, defeat ISIS, fair trade policies, repeal and replace the Affordable Care Act, rebuild the military). Toward the end of his speech he said, "It is time to show the whole world that America is back – bigger and better and stronger than ever before." Mr. Trump had big words, big plans, and big goals for what would come after a historic election.

People that I know and have worked with all over the country thought that Mr. Trump had a big corporate staff for all of his projects, subsidiaries, and companies. The reality is that Trump preferred a small staff partly because of cost, and because he thrived on internal competition among his staffers. His campaign staff was described as anything but big, and many wondered how he could compete against Clinton.

Often it was reported that he didn't have enough "boots on the ground." Less than a month before the presidential election, his campaign staff was skeletal, with 70 employees compared to hundreds for Clinton. He ran the campaign much like the Trump Organization, with a small team (Hope Hicks, Katrina Pierson, and Corey Lewandowski among others). His staffs may have been small but his vision, his plans, and his goals were big.

As a result of Trump's preference for small staffs, people who worked for him typically had more than one role and often did more than one job, unlike in other big companies with which I've been associated. For example, I was the corporate vice president of human resources for the Trump Hotel Collection and the local human resources executive at Trump International Hotel Las Vegas. On one occasion the Trump Hotel Collection corporate folks, including myself, were going to a meeting in Los Angeles that involved giving a presentation to some investors. I was speaking about our philosophy on hiring, orientating, and training staff. Our chief operating officer and VP of marketing were the only two individuals on the corporate payroll with offices in Trump Tower. Our COO, in advance of this meeting, secured corporate business cards for several of us, so that we could present them to the investors. Corporate business cards gave the perception that Mr. Trump had a corporate team working in New York solely on corporate projects. The truth is we did work on corporate projects – only not in Trump Tower.

Trump feeds off the belief that he does everything in a big way. Not having a big corporate staff might be perceived to mean that he could not afford one, but he would see that as fake news. Mr. Trump knew that if he hired the best people who had passion, drive, and enthusiasm, they would produce for him. And he promoted many people based on how well they did their jobs and on their loyalty to him. In *The Art of the Deal* he says, "The final key to the way I promote is bravado. I play to people's fantasies. People may not always think big themselves, but they can get very excited by those who do. That is why a little hyperbole never hurts. People want to believe that something is the biggest, the greatest, and the most spectacular."

Eunice Kennedy Shriver, sister to President Kennedy, rose to stardom by thinking big about intellectual disabilities and how they were perceived back in the late 1950s. She started with a simple idea that eventually became the Special Olympics. One Kennedy sister, Rosemary, was born with severe intellectual disabilities, and Eunice wanted to change how mental retardation, as it was called then, was treated and/ or ignored. In her back yard in 1962 she started a Camp Shriver so that people with intellectual disabilities could take part in sports and physical activities. Eunice believed that those with intellectual disabilities should have the same opportunity as anyone else. Her small camp soon blossomed into the first International Summer Olympics at Soldier Field in Chicago in July, 1968. In her speech at the first Special Olympics, "She pledged 'that this new organization, Special Olympics, would offer people with intellectual disabilities everywhere 'the chance to compete and the chance to grow.'"[1] In 1969, Eunice moved to France with her husband, Sargent Shriver, after he was appointed our ambassador there. In France she worked with organizations to develop activities for families with special needs children. This laid the foundation for the expansion of the Special Olympics around the world.

Eunice's small idea and commitment to a cause dear to her became something big. The 50ᵗʰ anniversary of the Special Olympics took place in 2018 in Chicago, where it had all begun. Eunice was posthumously awarded the Arthur Ashe Courage Award in 2017. That award, first given in 1993, is presented each year to individuals whose contribution goes well beyond sport. In 2006, Eunice Shriver received the designation DSG (Dame of the Order of St. Gregory the Great), a papal knighthood, from Pope Benedict XVI. Today, more than 4.7 million people in 170 countries participate in the Special Olympics. President Kennedy died five years before the program's official start, but his administration began to push legislation dealing with mental disabilities, helping to bring the subject out of the darkness. Since Eunice' death in 2009, her son Timothy has taken the reigns and continues the big work that his mother began over fifty years ago.

In the hotels that Trump envisioned, created, built, and managed during my time working for him, he would describe certain items, such as the building itself, as the tallest, or the size of the TV as the biggest, or the first-class appliances as the most spectacular. He used those and similar terms to describe his vision for America, for the people in America, for veterans, the active duty military, police, and first responders, and for the forgotten man and woman. He was on the world stage and he needed the world's attention. It doesn't get any bigger. And the people who ultimately supported him and voted for him were taking it all in during the many months that he campaigned across the country.

The thing that amazes me about his campaign for the presidency is that in addition to articulating his big goals for the country, he convinced the voters that he would be the one to accomplish them. Over and over in his rallies he told the crowd that if he was elected, "The chaos and violence on our streets ... if I am elected president, this chaos and violence will end – and it will end very quickly."[2] While he stumped for Republican candidates during the 2018 midterm elections, he told the crowds waving signs saying "Promises Made Promises Kept," that he had delivered on more things than he originally promised. President Trump may have signed bills and done some things he had not promised to do; however, not all of his promises have been kept. It is more than a year after the murder of 17 people at a High School in Parkland, Florida. Because guns and gun control are always a controversial topic, this should be one of the president's big priorities. Many Americans are waiting for some type of reform as innocent people are killed all over America in mass shootings. Little has been said by President Trump in the months since Parkland. In his remarks on February 15, 2018, a day after the massacre, Trump stated "making our schools and our children safe will be our top priority...." The student survivors are taking action on their own via Twitter, many tweeting that Trump, the candidate, accepted over $30 million for his presidential campaign from the National Rifle Association, and tweeting "Shame on you." President Trump believes in the right to bear arms and campaigned heavily on supporting that right. In Las Vegas the deadliest gun massacre in United States history occurred on October 1, 2017, with 58 people losing their lives and hundreds hospitalized. The presidents' supporters, like him, believe that guns get into the wrong hands and that that is the problem.

I marveled when Trump the candidate used inflated rhetoric about the other candidates during television interviews and in the presidential debates. He employed his own strange vernacular, slang, and nicknames of others to prop himself up. Apparently, Trump is a big fan of nicknames, and takes pride in telling others that he comes up with them himself! Perhaps most memorable was his reference at one of the debates to Senator Marco Rubio of Florida as "Little Marco." Rubio, who was seen early on as a viable contender, shot back a day later, on March 4, 2016: "He is taller than me – he's like six-two, which is why I don't understand why his hands are the size of someone who is five-two. Have you seen his hands? And you know what they say about men with small hands – you can't trust them." Of course, Trump had a typical Trump retort which was: "Look at my hands. Are those small hands? He said that if my hands are small, something else must be small. I guarantee there's no problem." This type of talk during a presidential campaign became a feast for cable news networks, radio shows, Twitter and the like. In the process Trump received hours on end of news coverage.

Throughout her career Mother Teresa received a lot of media coverage. To my mind, she and her Missionaries of Charity did more about poverty awareness and caring for the poor than anyone else in our time. Every president starting with Lyndon Johnson spoke of the poor and ridding the country of poverty. LBJ's "Great Society"[3] which started the Head Start program and what is commonly referred to as food stamps, unfortunately only perpetuated the plight of the poor. Research has shown that, more than fifty years after those programs began, poverty statistics are much the same.

Mother Teresa was born in Kosovo in 1910. Her father died when she was eight and she became interested in a religious life as a young girl. To learn English, she left for Ireland at 18 and joined an abbey. From there she moved to India at age 20, and never left. Teresa became a nun and took her final vows in 1937 while she was teaching school in eastern Calcutta, where she worked for almost two decades. She was particularly disturbed by the plight of the poor, which was worsened by the Bengal famine of 1943. According to Teresa, on a train trip from Darjeeling to Calcutta for a retreat she was told "I was to leave the convent and help the poor while living among them. It was an order. To fail would have been to break."[4] She went on to change her traditional habit to a cotton white sari that had a blue border, which is how her order of nuns is recognized. She ventured into the slums, ministering to the poor and sick while opening schools and hospitals. Early on, she and her followers begged for supplies to help the poorest among the poor, and in 1950 the Vatican granted her permission to create the religious order which became Missionaries of Charity. The order, in addition to taking the vows of chastity, poverty, and obedience, professed to give, wholeheartedly, free service to the poorest of the poor. Mother Teresa said her order would care for "the hungry, the naked, the homeless, unloved, uncared for throughout society...."[5] A hospice was opened in 1952, followed by another specifically for patients with leprosy, as well as outreach clinics throughout Calcutta. By 1960 her group was receiving worldwide attention, new sisters were joining and donations were coming in. The order she had founded was now represented around the world and Mother Teresa traveled the globe.

By 1996, there were 517 missions in more than 100 countries. The original group of nuns rose from 12 to thousands, with the first US presence being established in the Bronx, New York. Mother Teresa herself suffered health issues including two heart attacks in the 1980s and pneumonia in 1991, followed by a bout with malaria, then heart failure and heart surgery. She resigned as the matriarch of Missionaries of Charity in March 1997 and died in September at 88 years of age. More than 15,000 people attended her funeral, while millions flooded the streets of Calcutta to pay their final respects. In 1979 Mother Teresa was presented with the Nobel Peace Prize. She gave the commencement speech at Harvard University in 1982, and President Reagan presented her with the Presidential Medal of Freedom at the White House in 1985. She visited other US cities and one of my brothers and my mom were fortunate enough to meet her during that time. Mother Teresa was known for her profound quotes, one of which is "God doesn't require us to succeed, he only requires that you try."

This frail, soft-spoken woman spent her entire life serving the poorest of the poor, and she died among them. Her mission began with a goal of living the religious life, and that propelled her to think big and do great things. Already well-known at the time of her death, she rose to prominence in the Catholic world and moved rapidly along the path to sainthood. Mother Teresa was canonized a saint by Pope Francis on September 4, 2016.

My mom was in the moderate stages of Alzheimer's at the time of Mother Teresa's death, and was not aware that she had died or been canonized. Sometimes, toward the end of her life, I would say to her, "Mom, you met a saint." That meeting was a highlight of her life.

Before I left the Trump Hotel Collection to care for my mom, Mr. Trump had been thinking about acquiring a site in Washington, D.C. The old Post Office, built in 1892, was used for that purpose until 1914. After that it served as a federal office building until it was slated for demolition in the 1920s. It was not demolished, as it was considered a historic building, and during the 1970s and '80s it was renovated, adding retail space and a food court. In March of 2011 a request for proposals was issued by the General Services Administration, and ten bids were received. Most were for hotels, including a bid from Hilton Worldwide. On February 6, 2012, the GSA chose the Trump Organization as the potential redeveloper. The plan called for a $200 million project to include a 250-room luxury hotel with a conference center, spa, and three high-end restaurants. Much of the investment was in cash, not debt. Trump pledged to create a "small" museum dedicated to the history of the building. In the end, by June of 2013, the Trump Organization negotiated a 60-year lease, paying $250,000 a month in rent with increases tied to the consumer price index.

The hotel, which opened in October, 2016, is doing record business and has far surpassed all financial expectations. It has, however, become the subject of numerous lawsuits by watchdog groups and others including those who tried to have the liquor license revoked. A group of clergymen, including two rabbis, as well as two retired judges, filed a complaint in June, 2018, asserting that the liquor license violates a local law requiring the licensee to be "of good character." They are asking the District of Columbia Alcoholic Beverage Control Board to pull the Trump liquor license, asserting that "Mr. Trump put his character at issue when he certified that he is the owner of the licensee ... if he doesn't want to adjudicate his own character, he can transfer the ownership (of the liquor license) to someone who, as opposed to Mr. Trump, can meet the statutory requirements." They go on to say that "through his behavior both before and during his presidency, Donald J. Trump has demonstrated that he lacks good character. Good character involves an evaluation of an individual's moral and ethical qualities...."

A Washington, D.C. advisory neighborhood commission joined the petition in June, 2018. It begs the question, what is the difference between Trump being granted the license before he became president as opposed to after? Was he not considered to be of good character when the license was given? Late in July, 2018, President Trump lost his bid to throw out another lawsuit on whether or not the Trump D.C. Hotel business violates the Constitution, particularly as he is both the landlord and the tenant. Attorneys general in Washington and Maryland brought this suit, arguing that Trump is breaking the Emoluments Clause of the Constitution. In essence, that clause prohibits top government officials, including the president, from receiving money from domestic and foreign governments. They argue that, because President Trump owns the property, he is profiting from revenues generated there by both domestic and foreign governments. This is the second time a judge has rejected President Trump's attempts to dismiss the case. D.C. Attorney General Karl Racine called the decision a "substantial step forward to ensure President Trump stops violating our nation's original anti-corruption laws."[6]

In an extensive review of the emoluments clause issued in late 2016, it was concluded that "Mr. Trump, as president-elect, appears to be on a direct collision course with the Emoluments Clause."[7] The authors of the review cite the fact that Trump's many business holdings and transactions between foreign states and the Trump empire makes it "a virtual certainty that many [of these holdings and transactions]would create the risk of divided or blurred loyalties that the Clause was enacted to prohibit."[8] Things become even more muddled, they say, as the president refuses to make many of his business dealings transparent. And, even as President Trump delegated authority to his sons Donald Jr. and Eric to run the Trump Organization, he also involves them in federal business – for example, Donald Jr. having a role in interviewing candidates for the position of Secretary of the Interior. Mr. Trump's businesses owe millions to Deutsche Bank, the same organization that is negotiating a multi-million dollar settlement with the United States Department of Justice – of which the settlement will be overseen by an attorney general and others appointed by and serving at the pleasure of the president. In my opinion Mr. Trump, as a businessman and entertainer, had little idea of the intricacies of the office he was seeking when he announced his candidacy. Perhaps he did not take the time to learn, or listen to and consult with experts who might have steered him differently with respect to his businesses.

I can see how the lines are blurred. When I worked for Mr. Trump, his adult children ran the Trump Hotel Collection business and reported, as did I, to the chief operating officer. As the Trump International in Washington, D.C., is part of that business (now run by Don Jr. and Eric), and located in the president's back yard, it would be naïve to think that President Trump is not aware of what is going on there. A website even exists with daily updates on the comings and goings of all things Trump DC, even including health code violations. No president in history has been a businessman of his proportions, so it is likely that the Washington establishment is in a quandary about what to do. I also believe that because President Trump is so despised by many that they will take any action to undermine him, his agenda, and his businesses.

On the campaign trail and as president, Mr. Trump has used any opportunity he could to reference his properties, including the building project in Washington, D.C. At one rally in the summer of 2016, speaking about "Make America Great Again," Trump told the crowd that "it's gonna be the best hotel in Washington, D.C." During the first debate, he said that his D.C. hotel was "under budget, ahead of schedule, saved tremendous money." When Trump first announced his candidacy, he spoke over and over again about bringing America back bigger and better. When he spoke about his company or hotels, he said he was building on Pennsylvania Avenue, and that he was given the hotel project by the General Services Administration in Washington, noting "it was the most highly sought after – or one of them, but I think the most highly sought after project in the history of General Service ... Trump got it."

Trump also held press conferences at the hotel on live television, including in the days shortly before it opened. Beaming, he told the press, "I said this will be the best hotel in Washington. I think it may be one of the great hotels anywhere in the world." *Vanity Fair*, in writing a review of the hotel, said, "From the outside, it responds to a growing need, serves an audience, and looks quite grand. But on the inside, it is a complete disaster. Trump's new hotel, like his campaign, is a big idea followed by lazy execution."[9] In 2018, Trump International Washington D.C. earned a five-star rating from Forbes, which is a feat in itself, as few hotels receive that accolade in the first year of operation. In the meantime, Sean Spicer, former press secretary and author of *The Briefing*, held his first invitation-only book event at Trump International Washington D.C. Sean Hannity, Judge Jeanine Pirro, and others who are pro-Trump frequent the Washington, D.C. property and post about their presence at the hotel, often showing photos taken with Donald Trump Jr. and other celebrities.

Say what you will about Mr. Trump, he is a shrewd businessman. I saw that up close and personal in my time with the Trump Hotel Collection. Whereas any other candidate would pay millions for television ads during the campaign, he likely spent little money, because he received free advertising for himself and his hotels, and by being controversial and unorthodox. He did it then and he does it today as president. He frequently appears on the Fox News Channel, as do his children. News personalities from Sean Hannity, who has interviewed both Don and Eric Trump, to Judge Jeanine Pirro, who frequently interviews Eric and his wife Lara, have been part of the public relations onslaught. Each of these hosts, who are vocally pro-Trump, often invite folks from the other side of the aisle to give their views. In the end, it amounts to PR for the president and his agenda. The same people (including, of course, the Trumps) take to Twitter to remark about anything and everything to do with Trump and current politics. There are Twitter accounts for "Stump for Trump" and "Women for Trump," and they have thousands of followers.

The use of Twitter by the president is one way he has thought big. In a matter of seconds, he can send a message that reaches millions of people, and he says it exactly how he wants to, in his own words and in his own style. I think many people endorsed and voted for Trump because he does think big and his big plans for America resonated with the average American. Many people were tired of business as usual and of politicians who got elected and did very little. President Trump's "Drain the Swamp" mentality, along with the creation of a government agency (which Jared Kushner is overseeing) to rid the government of inefficiencies, is how Mr. Trump has done business for decades. According to Trump, the bottom line goes back to basics – love what you do, begin with baby steps, learn from your mistakes and learn from others. Thinking big can mean anything from a young person in rural America dreaming of going to Harvard and succeeding in being accepted there, to a community organizer who was working as a bartender getting elected as the youngest member of the US Congress.

Discussions about dreams and big thinking can be fun, interesting, and creative. Most parents want their children to think and dream big, to become anyone they want to be. In business and politics there are many, many examples of people who started small but thought big. Among them are Bill Gates, Founder of Microsoft, the late Steve Jobs of Apple, and President Barack Obama. Companies that empower employees for success typically promote the idea of thinking big. One big idea can be worth millions and blow away the competition.

Questions for this topic:

- What does "think big" mean to you?

- Who comes to mind when I ask about a person who thinks big?

- What did it take for that person's big idea to come to fruition?

- Have you had a "think big" idea and, if so, what happened?

- What does one need, in addition to a big thought, to succeed?

- How did your parents encourage you to think big?

Chapter 7 Endnotes

[1] *History of Special Olympics*, https://www/SODE.ORG.org

[2] Campaign Rally, Charlotte Convention Center, Charlotte, NC, August 18, 2016.

[3] Great Society and Head Start Info.

[4] Mother Teresa, *Wikipedia, The Free Encyclopedia*

[5] Missionaries of Charity, *Wikipedia, The Free Encyclopedia*

[6] Blair Guild and Rebecca Shabad, "D.C., Maryland announce they're suing Trump over foreign payments to his business," *CBS Interactive Inc.*, June 12, 2017.

[7] Norman Eisen, Richard Painter, and Laurence H. Tribe, "The Emoluments Clause: Its text, meaning, and application to Donald J. Trump," *Brookings Report*, December 16, 2016.

[8] Ibid.

[9] Emily Jane Fox, "Trump's D.C. Hotel is a Frightful Dump – and a Scary Metaphor for the Trump Presidency," *Vanity Fair*, November 10, 2016.

Chapter 8

Rules of Engagement
Work-Life Balance

There are only three measurements that tell you nearly everything you need to know about your organization's overall performance: employee engagement, customer satisfaction, and cash flow

~ Jack Welch

I chose to quote Jack Welch, former CEO of General Electric, as he has long been admired by Mr. Trump and additionally is one of the top business leaders of our time. In today's vernacular, Jack "gets it." Trump the businessman also gets it, albeit in a different style. Trump needed to know what guests and employees thought and based on that information how engaged they were with his brand. As he was/is obsessed with ratings and awards, it's not surprising that engaging his audience was high on the agenda.

In the almost five years of my Trump career, we did not spend money utilizing external companies to conduct employee surveys. Part of the reason was that we were growing rapidly and the staffs at the individual properties were small. That meant hotel leadership was tasked with keeping tabs on employee engagement. Years ago, it was referred to as employee satisfaction, which was then coined employee engagement. My experience has been that employee engagement at the time a property opens is relatively high. Everything is new, people typically have the tools and resources to do their jobs, and they are excited about the future. At Trump we had the finest of everything, pay was in many cases the highest in the cities where we were doing business, and benefits were competitive. Leaders walked the property daily and talked to employees as well as guests. When a guest had an issue, regardless of who they brought it to, the expectation was that it would be resolved before their departure. (Of course, there are some issues that cannot be fixed that rapidly or at all; however, a prompt response is the goal.) The same was true of employee concerns.

When Mr. Trump or one of his kids was coming to the property, the level of employee engagement was high. I particularly remember one time when Ivanka came to Las Vegas after the opening. The general manager told everyone in advance that Ivanka had requested to tour the entire building, including the office areas; she also wanted to meet the staff. She made certain she visited every department of the property and we were able to take photos with her. She was very lovely and engaging and we appreciated that she took the time to meet the employees. To some people that was the highlight of their career. People often enjoy meeting the leaders of the company for which they work. Particularly in large companies, the leaders are only known from photos on a wall. Most employees want to see the people at the top. In our case, albeit by video, we ensured that from day one every employee saw and heard Mr. Trump and his kids speaking to them. The video commanded employee attention. The Trump kids knew that in their hotels, golf courses, and other places where they depend on guests to pay the bills, employees must believe in the brand and be enthused about it. To start out enthusiastic and to stay enthused, in any company, takes work. Employee enthusiasm cannot be taken for granted.

During a trip to Trump Tower in New York, where we held the first leadership conference after the Trump Hotel Brand was launched, Mr. Trump was one of our scheduled presenters. There were approximately 30 of us, a relatively small group who were involved in the start of the brand – the hotel general managers, chief financial officers, and those of us with a corporate title responsible for finance, human resources, or marketing. Mr. Trump came into the room and immediately commanded everyone's attention. His presence and stature can be intimidating. Of course, he adores the stage and speaking from it. In this venue, he sat at the head of the large u-shaped table everyone was seated at, and all eyes were on him. After making some remarks about the brand and business in general, he asked if anyone had questions. (We had given our COO questions in advance that could be planted in the event no hands went up to ask Trump a question.) He was asked about expansion plans for the Trump Hotel Collection brand. At the time, global plans included Dubai and the now opened Trump Golf Course in Scotland. While I was still employed with Trump, the Dubai venture was started and anticipated to be quite a project. Unfortunately, however, it didn't happen.

Mr. Trump absolutely loves speaking to groups and large crowds, the bigger the better. In our case, we were his employees, so he talked most about the Hotel Collection, how proud he was of the brand, and the quality of the properties and products. He is not a shy man and he was just as boastful about his achievements then as he is now. At the time, I enjoyed the confidence with which he spoke, the pride that he had in the brand, in his kids, and in the fact that he took the time to take questions and engage us in the process.

Seeing Mr. Trump speak in person is engagement personified. He is obviously passionate about his company and he holds the attention of his listeners. When you think about it, he did what every CEO should be doing as part of their job: promoting the brand. And we were the people responsible for making or breaking the guest experience, so we listened to every word. The culture we created had a mission and vision statement whereby employees and guests were recognized, cultivated, and appreciated. By the same token, Mr. Trump was all business. He never, during the time I was employed, engaged in small talk with us. I do not recall ever hearing him ask any of us about anything personal or about our families. He did ask questions specifically about the hotels in which the executives worked. I really think, based on his personality, that during business hours he focused strictly on business. After hours, which we were not a part of, he is probably more engaging. In fact, the general manager at Trump Las Vegas, when he was Mr. Trump's bodyguard, related stories of traveling the world with Mr. Trump, going on his personal plane, attending Yankee games and so on. He had a lot of fun with Mr. Trump and whoever was in Trump's circle at the time.

Mr. Trump has said, "The Trump Hotel Collection has taken the Trump Organization international in a short amount of time. It was a natural extension of our brand ... and Donald Jr., Ivanka, and Eric have taken the concept worldwide. It has been exciting to see the growth and success of this collection."[1] I can imagine how much pride, as a businessman and a father, he has in his children, not to mention the confidence he must have in his sons to take over the task of leading the Trump Organization while he's not at the helm.

The best example for me of an engaging leader is the late Herb Kelleher, co-founder of Southwest Airlines. Not only did he revolutionize air travel, he did it in a creative and fun way that totally engaged his employees and customers. Herb once said "I don't believe that you have to be boring to be successful."[2] Herb earned degrees in English and philosophy and a Juris Doctor degree from New York University. While an undergraduate, he met his future wife, who was from Texas, and they eventually moved there. Herb intended to start a law practice, but after meeting a Texas businessman, they decided to found an airline. The initial concept was to connect up the Texas triangle with a low-cost air service. After several years of challenges and setbacks, the first Southwest flight took off on June 18, 1971.

"Kelleher's outrageous personality created a corporate culture which made Southwest employees well known for taking themselves lightly but their jobs seriously."[2] Herb's philosophy was employees come first, then customers and shareholders. He understood that engaged employees treat the customer well and invite them to return, which makes everyone happy. His style was very hands-on, walking and talking with employees and encouraging creativity. He admitted he knew nothing about running an airline but he knew about people and doing things that were non-traditional. Schools study Herb's management philosophy and countless companies have tried to copy Southwest's culture. (For me, the closest a CEO has come to emulating Herb is John Legere of T-Mobile. His zany antics, unconventional look, bold backing of his employees, and unparalleled customer service have engaged millions of customers.) In Herb Kelleher's case, "The airline continues to thrive in part because it hasn't veered from his original ideas of how to run a business."[4] Herb remained CEO and president of Southwest through February 2001 and then served as chairman of the board. He resigned from that role and the board of directors in 2008. Herb died on January 3, 2019, at age 87. "But his legacy extends far beyond our industry and far beyond the world of entrepreneurship. He inspired people; he motivated people; he challenged people – and, he kept us laughing all the way."[5] It is not surprising to me that Southwest Airlines consistently ranks in the top tier of best places to work in the United States [6] and for customers, the #2 airline in 2018.[7]

On the campaign trail, Trump's engagement was evident at his rallies and speeches. People in his base were enthused just by knowing he would be in or near their hometown, and they became more engaged after attending a rally. All we had to do was watch it live on television to see this. Early on, pundits were quite negative about Trump the campaigner. Michael Horn wrote, "Trump supporters lag behind Republican primary voters in general in high-engagement voter categories ... conversely, he enjoys a significant concentration of support among unengaged voters."[8] Mr. Trump found a way to, as he often says, bring the forgotten man and woman onto his team, his movement. Part of his strategy involved getting the base engaged with his vision of how to "Make America Great Again." At every opportunity he promoted his vision and spread his message to the people. After a while, my twin nephews, aged seven at the time, could repeat Trumpisms such as "You know it, I know it, and everybody knows it." He directly appealed to the voters' emotions and engaged with the audiences in every city, stadium, restaurant, factory, and workplace he visited. He was, after all, an entertainer and a salesman. And as a non-politician he had to sell the American people on why he was the only choice for voters in first the primaries and caucuses, and then the general election.

In the early days of his campaign I heard many comments that he would never last. I live in a blue state and many Trump supporters were not vocal about who they supported. I believe that is a reason why the pollsters got it wrong. People who supported Trump and remained silent helped to create the belief that Clinton was a shoe-in. Then, one by one, his bombastic, self-aggrandizing style defeated each of his fourteen well qualified Republican opponents. Mr. Trump spoke often about his energy, during his speeches and at the Republican debates. One thing you can say is that he was consistent in his talking points concerning himself, the other candidates, and some of the issues.

Energy, enthusiasm, and engagement went hand in hand for Mr. Trump. He understood, as a former Reality TV star, that people want to be entertained and excited. He more often than not spoke extemporaneously at his rallies, and his remarks often became the next news headline. In a campaign speech in New Hampshire on January 5, 2016, Trump commented about Hillary Clinton, "She has the biggest Teleprompters I've ever seen." The remark intimated that Ms. Clinton was old and may have had poor eyesight, hence the need for big teleprompters. It was classic Trump.

When people and pundits questioned his style or lack of presidential demeanor, it only emboldened him. He was speaking the way a lot of the American people spoke. In business, he has often indulged in bluster. In interviews he would say things that were bold or not politically correct because he cared about his supporters and not what the establishment thought about him, and he was quite successful. He does not fit any mold. But I can tell you this: people always knew exactly where they stood with Mr. Trump. He did not hold back or pull punches. If he was displeased with something at one of his properties, the person in charge was told immediately. Or if he wanted something in a property that others had doubts about, well, guess who won? When Trump International New York was undergoing renovation, the then general manager, Suzie Mills, questioned Mr. Trump about the size of the televisions he wanted to put in the guest rooms. Suzie thought 55-inch TVs were too big. The televisions were placed in the rooms. Suzie noted in a June 2010 interview with *Hotelier of the Week* that Ivanka, with whom she was working on the renovation,

"...has a different vision than her father, of style and taste, and it was very much the case of bringing the hotel in line with what's happening in the market in the moment." Those things included flat screen TVs and Blu-ray players.

"Engagement ultimately boils down to emotional connections between organizations and their employees ... this, in turn, generates positive influences on employee behavior, drive and work ethic."[9] When employees feel valued for who they are and how their contributions matter, they are more inclined to do good work and to speak highly of their companies. Today, with everything from Facebook to Twitter to Glassdoor, employees are posting reviews of their work places for others to see. Much like customer reviews on websites for restaurants and hotels, you can bet that companies with cultures like Southwest and T-Mobile are taking notice. To start a company or a brand and to maintain and enhance it and its culture takes much work. Starting on the right foot, incorporating humor and fun, has proven to work for these two companies. It is possible and it changed the corporate landscape in airlines and telecommunications for the better, in my opinion. For anyone who has been a Southwest Airlines customer, you see it in action with, predominantly, the flight attendants. For those customers of T-Mobile, I invite you to follow John Legere on Twitter. Whether it is he or his team that answers tweets, the reality is they are answered and whatever the issue is, it gets resolved and resolved quickly. Their "T-Force" of customer service gurus makes it fun to tweet with, and the customer service reps are dedicated to first acknowledging the customer, then understanding the problem or issue, and thanking the customer for their business while the issue is being taken care of. To say they are engaged and that they know how to engage the customer is an understatement.

Mr. Trump delivered the goods in his hotels. In *The Art of the Deal* Trump says, "You can't con people, at least not for long. You can create excitement, you can do wonderful promotion but if you don't deliver the goods, people will eventually catch on." Two months into his presidency, those not supporting Trump were already lamenting that he did not deliver the goods, specifically noting the failure to repeal the Affordable Care Act. Part of Trump's enthusiasm, in my opinion, is that he overpromises. He said many times on the campaign trail that he would repeal and replace Obamacare on day one of his presidency. Everyone knew that that would not happen, as he could not with the stroke of a pen repeal Obamacare. Furthermore, even today he and his administration have not outlined what their plan looks like. Occasionally, the president will make a remark that healthcare will be great and affordable, but the lack of specificity has been a problem for many. Simply stating that Obamacare is imploding or too expensive is not enough. Enthusiasm for an idea or product is essential; however, statements that cannot be backed up or are inaccurate can lead to disaster. It is a similar situation with building the wall. That campaign promise is still his goal, and some in the media say that his reelection depends upon it. Ann Coulter, who early on supported Trump to the point of predicting his election, has reversed course and is denouncing him for his inability to get funding for the wall. He was adamant on the campaign trail and in the early days of his presidency that Mexico would pay for the wall. He has vacillated on that issue and backed down to the point that he has asked Congress for the money. There still exists enthusiasm among his base, but many Trump supporters and resistors alike believe he will not be re-elected, based on unfulfilled promises such as the wall.

President Trump already has his talking points handy when the pundits attack him on this theme. He will say that it is the Democrats who are resisting and battling him at every turn, and to a great extent that seems to be true. Candidates running for any office, including the presidency, often make promises they cannot keep. The American people are used to it and often we cut the person some slack, particularly if it is someone we voted for. So, we will have to see how the enthusiasm for President Trump plays out, and what remaining promises will be fulfilled while he launches his "Keep America Great" campaign.

Engaging his audience, be it at a rally, a meeting with heads of state, or with businesspeople, is something Trump is crafty about. He often, even when using prepared remarks and a teleprompter, goes off script and uses humor to engage the audience. At one televised event, he actually threw pages of notes into the air so he could speak extemporaneously. In his two-hour plus speech at the CPAC Conference in March, 2019, Trump said to the audience, "You know I'm going off script ... going off script is how I got elected." I think this is another attribute that so many people like about him – the ability to do something that is unpresidential. It is Trump being Trump, and I don't believe that will ever change. His enthusiasm about himself, his ideas, and his agenda is plain for the world to see. He is engaging even when the topic is negative, so that he can get buy-in from his constituencies. He has the uncanny ability to engage folks whom he personally attacked and disparaged in the primaries. It is essential that the Republicans who were not on board with him in 2016 get on the Trump train to ensure a Republican victory in 2020.

Mr. Trump was successful in engaging people who were

on his reality television shows, *The Apprentice* and *Celebrity Apprentice*. Folks clamored to become contestants and competed hard for the chance to win. He used his bravado and penchant for competitiveness to engage the contestants and the audience, including his famous phrase, "You're fired," which became a Trump trademark. Whatever you want to say about him, he utilizes the skills and attributes he possesses to his advantage. Michael D'Antonio, a Trump biographer, said "Anyone who engages with the President and, before that, with him as a businessperson, had to practice self-defense even if they were his allies ... all that matters to him is what you say and do in the moment [you are]in front of him."[10] We learn at a young age that if we cannot say something nice about a person, we should say nothing at all. I believe most voters would say that they expect a president to have a high moral compass. Unfortunately, there are dozens of instances in which, in tweets or interviews, he has not been able to hold his tongue. As a businessman, saying anything and everything he wanted, including shocking statements, was okay. However, as president, resorting to name-calling and character attacks is not constructive. It does not help the party, the base, or the country. These traits are unacceptable and irresponsible and not befitting a president. People do not forget when they are disparaged or ridiculed, and that could come back to haunt President Trump as he forges ahead with his re-election campaign.

When discussing engagement, whether it is with students, volunteers or business colleagues, it imperative to know certain things:

- First and foremost, know your audience. Students

144

define engagement in a very different way than, for example, business leaders do.

- Second, inquire from the group what behaviors of engagement look like to them.

- Third, in the demographic you are training or speaking with, have examples ready of those people who are deemed engaging, and discuss their attributes.

- Ask why a certain person or persons are found to be engaging.

- Discuss what it takes for a person to engage with their audience, peers, supervisors.

- Discuss how we teach people, from children to seniors, to be more engaging.

Chapter 8 Endnotes

[1] Donald J. Trump with Meredith Mciver, *Think Like a Champion,* (New York: Vanguard Press, 2009).

[2] "Kelleher: Southwest Has Never Furloughed an Employee – Here's Why," *www.wsj.com/.../southwest-airlines-co.founder-herb dies at 87*

[3] "Herb Kelleher" *Wikipedia*

[4] Matt Grossman, "Forever Herb: The Laughs, The Leadership, The Legacy," *Southwest the Magazine*, March, 2019.

[5] Jackie Wattles, "Herb Kelleher, Southwest Airlines founder, dies at 87," *www.cnn.com/...business/southwest-airlines-founder...*

[6] Best Places to Work in the US, Glass Door Survey, 2018.

[7] Julian Mark Kheel, "The Best and Worst US Airlines in 2018," March 6, 2018.

[8] Michael Horn, Contributor, "The Unengaged and Uninformed," *U.S. News & World Report,* September 1, 2015

[9] Andrew Hazelton and Matt Peterson, "Hotels Can't Afford to Ignore This Employee Benefit," February 18, 2019, https://lodgingmagazine.com/hotels-cant-afford-to-ignore-this-employee-benefit/

[10] Peter Baker and Maggie Haberman, "For Many, Life in Trump's Orbit Ends in a Crash Landing," *New York Times,* April 26, 2018.

Chapter 9

Brand – You, Your Company, Your Reputation
Values Matter

If your business is not a brand, it is a commodity
                                    ~ Donald J. Trump

A few years after I reentered the workforce, I had the occasion to give a short presentation on "branding." In the discussion, I asked participants to shout out names of famous brands. The companies mentioned were Nike, Pepsi, and Mercedes Benz, among others. Then I asked them to tell me if they could remember the tag line or logo for the brand. Without a doubt, Nike's "Just do it" won hands down. We then talked about the particular brand and, when they heard the brand name, what first came to mind. When I talked about my Trump experience, we discussed how Trump, the brand, connotes luxury, elegance, wealth, and a certain lifestyle that many aspire to achieve. For me it was interesting that the other notable brands mentioned (Nike, Pepsi, Mercedes Benz, Ralph Lauren, etc.) spend millions of dollars on advertising in magazines and on television. I asked if anyone recalled seeing a television ad for anything Trump. The answer was a resounding no – why? Because Mr. Trump gets free advertising from being on television and radio and will use those avenues, regardless of what he is speaking about, to advertise or promote his own products. In a *Time* magazine article Jeffrey Kluger says "There's the compulsive promotion of the Trump name ... but the Trump name is everywhere in the Trump world."[1]

While newly employed at the Trump Organization and before we watched *The Apprentice*, my mom and I talked about Mr. Trump. I wanted to know what her perception of him was. The first thing she mentioned was that "he sells steaks on one of the shopping channels." At the time Mom, who was almost 80, read three newspapers a day, and she was aware that Trump was frequently in the news. Mom also watched *Larry King Live*, where Mr. Trump was a frequent guest. In fact, Mom called me every time Trump was on the show to say, "Your boss is on

TV." Mom lived about an hour or so from Mar-a-Lago, so the local papers often had articles about anything associated with the country club or golf course. All these years later I can still hear Mom's voice saying, "Your boss is on TV."

That is part of Trump's branding genius. It began long before the 2007 media event announcing the name Trump Hotel Collection as his hotel brand. Mr. Trump said that the name was "a natural extension of our brand in the luxury sector of the hotel industry."[2] There is no argument that Trump has made millions selling his name on products, services, and buildings. He has been given royalties for his men's ties, for books, and for many other products. In his revised edition of *Great Again* Mr. Trump says, "I also knew that the Trump brand is one of the world's great icons of quality and excellence ... everybody knows about it." And, if by chance they don't, he makes sure they do. Prior to my mom's Alzheimer's becoming debilitating, my brother and I took her to Italy, where at the age of 80 she met her cousins for the first time. When I spoke of my career and who I worked for, I would say the "Trump Hotel Collection." People would invariably then ask, "Donald Trump?" His name, which is his brand, is known worldwide. This was long before he had vast holdings outside of the U.S., and years before he announced his candidacy for the presidency. People would marvel at the fact that they were now speaking to someone who worked for someone famous. The significance of branding cannot be overstated.

Richard Branson, who started a magazine as a teenager, built and turned Virgin Group into one of the best and largest brands of our time. Born in England in1950, he became a self-made man starting with his *Student* magazine which he initially envisioned at the age of 15. The first edition was published when he was 18. Even though he had dyslexia and performed poorly at school, he followed in his mother's footsteps and became an entrepreneur. He has said that both of his parents were very creative about ways to make money, and he followed in their footsteps. Upon finishing his studies, his headmaster said, "Congratulations, Branson. I predict that you will either go to prison or become a millionaire."[3] Branson never went to college and says this was a blessing, as he believes he never would have started his company had he done so. He used his magazine to interview famous personalities including, among others, Mick Jagger of the Rolling Stones and John Lennon, and also to advertise their records. At 20 years old he set up a mail order business selling records for less than the stores, followed by a chain of record stores branded Virgin Records. By 1972, at age 22, he had 14 record shops. The brand took off and in the 1980s he created Virgin Atlantic Airline. He has dabbled in many other industries including several that failed. Of that he says, "I suppose the secret to bouncing back is not only to be unafraid of failures but to use them as motivational and learning tools ... There's nothing wrong with making mistakes as long as you don't make the same ones over and over again."[4]

Branson has launched dozens of businesses and hundreds of small companies. He has written numerous books, starting with one in 1998 that told the story of how he went from a small magazine publisher into one of the biggest brands of our time. Many of his own books were published under Virgin Publishing. In March, 2000 Branson was knighted by the Prince of Wales at Buckingham Palace for his achievements as an entrepreneur. Of his knighthood he said that he was accepting it on behalf of all his employees. "They have all worked very hard to make Virgin what it is and I am accepting this honour on behalf of them."[5] In 2004 Branson started his "Virgin Unite" philanthropic association which includes initiatives to address homelessness and poverty. He "publicly commits to give away half of his fortune to philanthropic causes."[6]

Most recently he wrote *Finding my Virginity,* which he described as "The story of the last two decades, told through one of the most dynamic brands in the world."[7] In 2018, his Virgin brand entered the Las Vegas market when he bought the Hard Rock Hotel Casino, then closed the property for a huge renovation and re-brand under his Virgin Hotels company. Branson's brand, Virgin, is iconic as is the man himself. He is a risk-taker, a pioneer, and a philanthropist who uses his brand to benefit himself, his employees, his customers, and his humanitarian efforts. Branson's philosophy is "Train people well enough so they can leave, treat them well enough so they don't want to."[8]As of April 2018, Branson's net worth is estimated at $5.1 billion. According to Forbes, he is the 286th richest person in the world.

There is little argument that few people anticipated Trump would receive the GOP nomination in 2016, and fewer still that he would be elected as our president. In September, 2016 self-made billionaire Mark Cuban tweeted, "If @realdonaldtrump loses this election, im [sic] betting he personally goes bankrupt w/in 7 yrs. That's how toxic his brand now is." In 2015, there were 19 companies that paid Trump to produce or distribute his goods. Before running for the presidency, Mr. Trump made millions selling his name for products from steaks to neckties to mattresses and water. He even had a fragrance called "Success" which he introduced at Macy's New York in 2012, while accompanied by the winner of the 2010 Miss Universe pageant. Since his election in 2016, politics has changed the

Trump merchandise brand, which is in decline. Royalties fell from more than $2.4 million to just over $370,000. Now most of the products are no longer on the market.

Of the seven hotels I helped open for the Trump Hotel Collection, three no longer bear the Trump name. Trump SoHo, a partnership with the Bayrock Group, which Felix Sater[9] worked for, terminated Trump's contract and paid fees to do so. Sater, who pleaded guilty to a stock fraud scheme in 1998 and served 15 months in prison, became an FBI informant. His association with Bayrock terminated in 2008 after Trump SoHo opened. The hotel went into foreclosure in 2013 and after Trump was inaugurated, closed one restaurant and was steadily losing customers.

"Red, blue, indifferent – every demographic has an easy excuse to stay anywhere other than a hotel bearing the Trump name."[10] It is interesting that in the city he grew up in and in which he undertook iconic real estate projects, the Trump name is quickly disappearing from the landscape. "Although their name will disappear from Trump SoHo, Robert Mueller is making sure that they can't really leave – at least not yet."[11]

Since election day, six buildings in New York that bear the Trump name announced that their residents had voted to remove the name. In February 2019, the sixth building's tenants said they would remove "Trump Place" from their building. "The condo board said that the president's company still holds a contract to manage the building, and the contract was not affected by the removal of the sign."[12] President Trump's name remains on nine buildings in Manhattan, including of course Trump Tower. Many retailers, including Macy's, dropped Trump merchandise in 2017. A corporate spokesperson for Macy's said, "We are disappointed and distressed by recent remarks about immigrants from Mexico." A Fox Business report from May 2018 stated that Trump's net worth had dropped $100 million since 2017, and that his net worth then was roughly $2.8 billion, with $520 million of debt.

After Trump called for a complete ban on Muslims entering the United States, a Dubai-based company that was licensed to sell Trump furniture stopped doing so. Several companies selling things like mattresses and pillows allowed their licenses to expire, citing slow sales. In Mr. Trump's 2017 financial disclosure form he reported royalties from licensed merchandise as $370,000 compared to millions from prior years. And, according to American University,[13] only two companies are still paying to put Trump's name on their merchandise. One is HomeStudio, which produces bed linens and housewares, and the other is Dorya, which produces Trump furniture.

Politics. Trump's politics have certainly changed the landscape in Washington, D.C. In fact, Donald J. Trump re-branded the Grand Old Party (GOP) right before everyone's eyes, and that helped to catapult him to the presidency. Ivanka Trump said to Breitbart, "From day one, my father set the agenda for what the whole party is talking about." Rob Frankel, a branding expert, said Trump took his tactics "right out of my playbook and I'm really proud of the way he did it ... he did exactly what everybody else should be doing for their brand. To be effective, you have to be clear, authoritative. And then there's my prime directive: for a brand to work it has to be perceived as the only solution." Candidate Trump believed that, and he managed to get the electorate to buy into his movement and his "Make America Great" brand. He proclaimed himself to be the solution to Hillary Clinton. He was the only one who could reform the immigration system, rebuild the military, and wipe

ISIS off the face of the earth. In a speech on September 3, 2016, candidate Trump said, "Becoming the nominee of the party of Abraham Lincoln has been the greatest honor of my life ... it is [with] his legacy that I hope to build the future of the party, but, more importantly, the future of the country."[14] During President Obama's second term the Republican Party basically ran on anti-Obama rhetoric and the repeal of Obamacare. The GOP had to convince the voters that it was still the party of Lincoln and Reagan.

The appearance of Trump's name in a newspaper article, a TV interview, on a building, or a book added value to his brand. The fact that Trump branded his political campaign very early on as "Make America Great" was no accident. In April of 2016, speaking about running for the presidency, he said, "We need someone who can take the brand of the U.S. and make it great again." He has transitioned Make America Great into his administration, from the twitter hashtag "MAGA" to the MAGA hats and everything in between. The man is a branding genius. The theme resonated with the average American. Trump utilized the negativity in America and the average citizen's disgust with politicians to create a MAGA vision for the country. Like his companies, which he describes as great, fantastic, or big league, so too with MAGA. He imagined great things for the American people and for the country. Mr. Trump did the same with his hotels: he wanted them to be the best, the greatest, the most luxurious. And not just for the guests, but for the outside entities that rate and assign stars and other accolades, of which he is extremely proud. He expects greatness from himself and from everyone who works for him.

Proctor & Gamble is an American multinational corporation that makes quality products for consumers and expects great things from its employees. I lived and worked in downtown Cincinnati, where P&G is headquartered, and had friends who worked there. Started in 1837 by two friends, one a candle-maker, the other a soap maker, the company became a dominant player for consumer goods and a place where people wanted to work. In 1887, after the success of Ivory soap, the company started a profit-sharing plan for employees to both create loyalty and keep them from going on strike. In the 1950s, when most women were moms and did not work outside the home, P&G dominated television ads during the daytime serials. They understood the audience and catered to them. In fact, the shows became known as "soap operas" because of the laundry soap advertisements. P&G quickly differentiated their laundry detergent, Tide, from brands like Cheer or Dash with their ads and brand marketing. They were diligent and precise in everything from the packaging, and its colors to the look and the price. In those days, brand reputation and loyalty were given and maintained through television and magazine ads. "Proctor & Gamble was the first one to discover the perfect recipe for laundry detergent ... P&G spent time and money ... the company would conduct shipping tests ... trying out strategies to select markets ... advertising in those markets, polling consumers about the product."[15] Today, P&G concentrates on 65 brands that produce 95 percent of their profit, and they continue to be the single biggest spender of advertising. In 2017, P&G spent $7.1 billion in advertising (television, print, radio, Internet and in-store).

Titans of industry spend millions of dollars paying top-notch public relations and advertising companies to assist them with their branding. Donald J. Trump did it with his name and his narcissism. While I was employed with the

Trump Organization, the company did pay for the services of professional advertising and public relations companies. But I am confident that Mr. Trump may have been responsible for more media exposure on his own than most clients. Going back to my time working for Trump, it was easy to recruit employees by just utilizing the Trump name, as it personifies excellence. I remember going to career fairs at the University of Nevada Las Vegas (UNLV). For the first event, during pre-opening, as we set up our area, I borrowed the sales department's banner, and we brought some glossy brochures and a video along with "Trump Ice" (bottled water). Anything with the Trump name people gravitated to. Our gift shop had a lot of high-end clothes, jewelry, and other items as well as Trump-branded merchandise, and that is what people wanted. When I went to Trump Tower in New York for the first time, I was amazed to be surrounded by all things Trump, including the Trump Gift Shop, Trump Café, and so on.

In his book *Think Like A Champion* Mr. Trump says, "I've been building the Trump brand for several decades ... having a quality brand is very much like having a good reputation ... the Trump brand has to represent the highest quality available, no matter what the enterprise might be." It was no different in hiring and training our staff. We had a blueprint for success that included a two-day orientation program with a video explaining the Trump Hotel Collection and Mr. Trump's expectations, core training programs for every employee (even those who did not interact with guests), and on-the-job training which detailed everything from the exact placement of amenities in the guest rooms to how to resolve a disputed mini-bar charge. It was absolutely not acceptable, when a guest said "thank you" for an employee to reply "no problem."

Trump's brand was not an informal one and our standards reflected as much. Mr. Trump and his children were well aware that everything from an employee's uniform to the words they spoke would be scrutinized by our clientele. I remember when I invited a former colleague to interview for the food and beverage management position. This individual had worked for luxury properties, was a Cornell graduate and had lots of experience in the hotel business. After he interviewed with the hotel general manager, I asked the GM for his feedback. The thing I recall most is the GM's remark that Mr. Trump would like his "look." Mr. Trump, he told me, likes beautiful (looking) people! I guess it's part ego and just good for business.

Mr. Trump was extremely particular and he expected to see well-groomed and well-spoken employees taking care of his guests. He was very proud of his brand and his brand's reputation. And every use of his brand (the Trump name), had to be exact – the placement, the logo, the style. Nothing was done haphazardly. Our marketing team, during pre-opening, was looking for a small token of appreciation for the invitees to our topping off ceremony. We settled on Trump-branded pens and travel shoe polishers, which was so appropriate since folks would have the occasion near the ceremony location to walk on or near sand (as the project was still under construction). Long after that event, we utilized the pens and shoe polishers at recruiting events and they went like hotcakes. I continued ordering them as giveaways during my entire tenure with the Trump Hotel Collection. For me, it was a subtle message to job applicants that one of our expectations was polished shoes. Wherever I go, even today, I notice things like that, and it's amazing to me that so many hospitality and service workers go to their jobs with inappropriate footwear or unpolished shoes.

In a CNBC interview in June 2011 entitled "I Love Making Deals," Trump was asked about the essence of building a brand. He responded, "Building a brand is very interesting. You need time, you need quality, you need success. You want to do something that's special, and people start following. And, when they start following, you've built yourself a brand." One of his quotes is, "If your business is not a brand, it's a commodity. Your business, and your brand, must first let people know what you care about, and that you care about them." This is what he reiterated over and over again on the campaign trail ... how he cared about the forgotten men and women of our country.

I see similarities in the White House, which is a different "brand" for President Trump. He has hired and promoted people who are adept at promoting the "MAGA" brand (Kellyanne Conway and Sara Sanders, for example). He has taken branding to a whole new level by holding rallies in states that he carried in order to tout whatever it is he is selling. He kicked off his 2020 re-election campaign in Melbourne, Florida in February, 2017. Signage for the event said, "We are going to put America back to work. We are going to put people before government." President Trump and many of his White House staff are on Twitter and Facebook sending weekly posts with updates and other information. The Facebook posts always end with a request for donations to the party. In one concerning an event President Trump was hosting at Mar-A-Lago, it included a chance to meet the president for anyone who donated even a dollar. One had to make a donation in order to enter the contest. Like many companies, the White House has a social media director, and I can only imagine how busy that person must be trying to keep up with the various social media sites and the president's tweeting.

But, getting back to Trump the businessman, some endeavors have been more successful than others. With just weeks remaining before the election, he found time to leave the campaign trail to attend his Washington D.C., hotel's grand opening, saying, "We're very proud of our company," and he later used the bully pulpit to promote the hotel. Mar-a-Lago, where Trump married Melania, is his Palm Beach resort, and often functioned as a satellite campaign office. Built in the 1920s, it is a 125-plus room, 63,500 square foot mansion with the separate Mar-a-Lago Club. Mr. Trump purchased the estate, which at the time was the largest mansion in the U.S., in 1985. Now Mar-a-Lago is the Presidents' winter White House where he conducts official business, holds cabinet meetings, and hosts heads of state. It is the second-largest mansion in Florida and the twentieth-largest in the United States. Federal law makes it legal for a president to designate a residence outside of the White House as a temporary office so that federal money can be allocated to provide necessary facilities there.

President Trump continues to brand his hotels, and he utilizes any and every opportunity to advertise them. He officially kicked off his re-election campaign with a fundraiser at his DC Hotel in June of 2017. He has spent numerous weekends at Bedminster, New Jersey (where he has a golf course), Mar-a-Lago, and most recently Scotland (where he has two golf courses) in advance of his meeting in Helsinki, Finland with Vladimir Putin. An article by journalist Katie Rogers stated that "Mr. Trump has, for the most part, ignored the large rallies against him in the United Kingdom, instead focusing on promoting Turnberry. He described it as magical on the world stage this past week."[16] The president golfed at both of the Scottish resorts that bear his name, and repeatedly mentioned Turnberry when speaking to the press. In a tweet while golfing at Turnberry, he said, "The weather is beautiful and this place is incredible!" Ms. Rogers wrote: "It is a tactic that has alarmed ethics watchdogs, who say he is using his presidential platform to promote a resort that, according to financial filings, has been a burden on the family business."[17]

Trump is a promoter, his name is his brand, and he is unlike any other person who has held the office of president. His second visit to Turnberry was the 169th time the president has visited a property owned, managed, or branded by his Trump Organization. Since his swearing in, the Trump Organization has profited by Secret Service and other personnel traveling to and staying at Trump properties.

When I was employed at the Trump Organization, Ivanka Trump launched a fine jewelry line using the Trump name. She partnered with a real estate and diamond heir and licensed her name for use by Madison Avenue Diamonds. Like her father, she has licensed the Trump name in exchange for royalties. That jewelry line became mired in lawsuits, and Ivanka terminated the relationship with her partner. Ivanka, much like her father (a Wharton Business School graduate) wrote a book, *The Trump Card: Playing to Win in Work and Life,* and she launched the Ivanka Trump Brand in 2011. Her former website said it is a brand launched by women for women, and included shoes, handbags, apparel, accessories, fashion jewelry, and baby bedding. In what I found a surprising move, Ms. Trump announced on July 24, 2018 that she is closing her namesake fashion brand. She said, "After 17 months in Washington, I do not know when or if I will ever return to the business, but I do know that my focus for the foreseeable future will be the work I am doing here in Washington ... so making this decision now is the only fair outcome for my team and partners." It appears that Ivanka will remain in Washington, D.C. as a part of President Trump's administration working to promote and pass her father's agenda. I imagine she views her role as a Senior Advisor to the President as more impactful than the Ivanka Trump brand, at least for now.

- For business training, lead a discussion by asking, "What is our brand?" The answers will give you insight into whether people know and understand what the brand is. If there is confusion or any misconception, you and your team should work on clearing that up. Or, perhaps the brand information is not consistent – which is something that can be worked on.

- After learning what people answer to "What is our brand?" follow up by asking, "What value does our brand represent?" To be viable and respected, a brand must provide value to the consumer. Whether it is a hospital, a car company, a hotel, or a college, value is inherently important to a brand. Without it, people will find a different brand that they associate with value.

- For people who are self-employed, ask yourself, what is my brand? Initially you may not know how to answer, or will answer with just an adjective or two describing yourself or your work. This can lead you to give more thought to how best to brand yourself and your business.

- In speaking with students, sport is a good way to begin a brand discussion. Each team in all professional leagues has a brand, and people relate to it or not. From a logo on a team cap or jersey to the tag line of the team or the merchandise they sell, it is or should reflect their brand.

- The brand discussion and/or training can morph into brand loyalty. Today more than ever, with all of the competition in every segment of society, loyalty is very important to a company's success. Advertising was once a key factor in brand loyalty, but no longer. Talk about what factors go into brand loyalty.

- Finally, discuss reasons people leave a brand. Include cases of advertisers leaving networks because of statements made by those on television that are offensive or not in keeping with a company's point of view. Brand loyalty, or joining or leaving a brand, also involves employees of a company, students of a college or university, and people who volunteer for a particular organization or nonprofit.

Chapter 9 Endnotes

[1] Jeffrey Kluger, "The Truth About Donald Trump's Narcissism," *Time Magazine*, August 11, 2015.

[2] Press Release: Introducing Trump Hotel Collection: The Next Generation of Luxury Hospitality, *Hospitality Net*, October 11, 2007.

[3] Richard Branson, *Finding My Virginity: How I Survived, Had Fun, and Made a Fortune Doing Business My Way* (New York: Crown Business, 1998.)

4 Richard Branson, Like a *Virgin – Secrets They Won't Teach You at Business School* (Virgin Books, 2013).

[5] "Virgin Tycoon is knighted," *BBC News,* Homepage| World Service| Education. March 30, 2000.

[6] Adam Sherwin, "Richard Branson is latest billionaire to join Bill Gates' $500bn philanthrophy club giving pledge," https://www.independent.co.uk

[7] Richard Branson, *Finding My Virginity* Prologue (New York: Penguin Group USA, 2017.)

[8] Richard Branson, *Finding My Virginity: How I Survived, Had Fun and Made a Fortune Doing Business My Way.*

[9] Felix Sater, *Wikipedia, The Free Encyclopedia.*

[10] Nikki Ekstein, "The Trump SoHo Hotel Was Struggling to Survive. Then It Dropped Its Name," *Luxury Travel*, February 27, 2019.

[11] Timothy O'Brien, "Trumps Can Never Really Check Out of SoHo Hotel," https://www.bloomberg.com/opinion/articles/2017-11-22/trumps-ditch-soho-hotel-but-not-robert-mueller

[12] David A. Fahrenthold and Jonathan O'Connell, "Condo Board in New York votes to remove 'Trump Place' from building," *Washington Post,* February 22, 2019.

[13] Kathryn Sanders, David A. Fahrenthold and Zane Anthony, "Trump's merchandising empire is over," *American University School of Communication,* April 12, 2018.

[14] Katie Rogers, "In Trump's U.K. Visit, some see 'Infomercial' for Money-losing Golf Resort," *New York Times,* June 14, 2018.

[15] "Here's Why Brand Loyalty is Not Totally Dead," https://socialmarketingsolutions.com/

[16] https://socialmarketingsolutions.com/

Chapter 10

Winning – Connecting the Dots
Gratitude, Generosity and Goodness

Winning isn't everything, but wanting to win is
> ~ Vince Lombardi

My whole life is about winning. I don't lose often. I almost never lose
> ~ Donald J. Trump

For many years Donald Trump has been saying a lot of things about the state of America, the American economy, trade practices, and how bad the country is doing. As a candidate for the presidency he vowed to the American people to "Make America Great Again." The questions are: can he do it, and what has he done since becoming president to make America great again?

First and foremost, he ran on a platform that he was not a politician. He believed that because he was a successful businessman, he could bring his business attributes (negotiating, deal-making), to Washington and fix all of the government's problems. He was going to get rid of the waste and corruption, and he would "drain the swamp." But rather than actually reducing the size of the government, he first has to make it more efficient, and he appointed Jared Kushner, his son-in-law, head of a new White House Office of American Innovation to do just that. This included the size of agencies, eliminating people or positions that do duplicative work, and vastly improving the information technology and internet security of the government agencies. We do know that many positions in the administration remain unfilled. Mr. Kushner rarely speaks; we see him occasionally with the president at a briefing or in a meeting. The landmark legislation regarding prison reform, which Kushner took the lead on, is the most talked about accomplishment in his role. The president will often say Kushner is doing a great job, but he seems to use that phrase frequently without any specifics except for the "Second Chance Act."[1]

President Trump's 100-day plan to make America great again called for, among other things, removing more than 2 million (Trump's number) criminal aliens from our country, cancelling every executive order issued by President Obama, suspending immigration from regions where vetting cannot safely occur, allowing the Keystone pipeline to proceed, lifting restrictions on fossil fuel production, selecting a Supreme Court nominee in the mold of the late Justice Scalia, canceling billions in payments to the United Nations' climate change programs, establishing a requirement that for every new federal regulation, two existing regulations must be eliminated, and ending federal funding for sanctuary cities. In the 2018 Omnibus Spending Bill, which he reluctantly signed, little money was appropriated for the border wall, which Trump had said Mexico would pay for. As Trump became more and more frustrated, he made the decision to get the military involved to support the border patrol personnel, and said he would place the National Guard on the border. Democrats were outraged by this decision and accusations of hatred and bigotry got louder and louder as some said Trump was trying to make America white again.

Trump campaigned on the notion that America has not been an exceptional nation or even a great one in recent decades, and that he alone could make it great again. For decades he has spoken about his views on trade, how the world has laughed at America, and how other countries have taken advantage of us by not paying their fair share to NATO and the UN. He said he was tired of America being ripped off, and that we have to be treated fairly by other countries. He reiterated that sentiment as recently as September, 2018 at his second address to the United Nations' General Assembly. Winning to businessman Trump meant, as I saw it, that his buildings had to be the best, the tallest, the most luxurious and built both ahead of schedule and under budget. Using these and similar superlatives, Trump would go on the airwaves and talk about winning. His attitude about winning permeated every facet of his life. Winning to Trump definitely involves affirming that he is doing a great job, and having others acknowledge it as well.

There are two groups who rate hotels and restaurants all over the world and recognize success by giving out "stars" or "diamonds." The Automobile Association of America (AAA) and *Forbes Travel Guide* are the organizations doing this today. Both lists represent the ultimate in luxury, service, and amenities. The winners usually include some of the world's most expensive accommodations. AAA and *Forbes* both do unannounced inspections and spend a night at the properties they are rating so that they can write detailed reports about the experience. AAA has a much larger full-time staff, while Forbes typically inspects current five-star recipients and those aspiring to be five-star. It is an extensive and time-consuming process covering even the smallest of details. Having worked in numerous hotels undergoing these inspections, I have participated in the feedback sessions; they are a gift to hoteliers, serving as blueprints for success. The report is very detailed, which permits the inspected hotel to know what issues need attention in order to achieve the desired result. These can include everything from employee behavior and interactions with guests to physical plant and maintenance issues.

When I first began working for the Trump Hotel Collection, the New York property held the five-star distinction. Mr. Trump was adamant about keeping it, because it meant winning. The New York property has received the Forbes Five-Star award for many years in a row. The New York property is the only one in New York City that has a five-star and five-diamond hotel and restaurant (Nougatine, managed by Chef

Jean George Vongerichten). On one of my trips to New York City, my mom met me there, and we were lucky enough to meet Chef Jean George and dine in his restaurant. He could not have been nicer. I do not remember what we ate or how we rated the meal as I preferred to observe the employees' behavior and level of service.

A few years after that visit with Mom, Mr. Trump decided to renovate the Trump International New York hotel guest rooms. The hotel had opened in 1997 and, while still luxurious, it was now dated. The press release noted that "the hotel completed its spectacular $30 million renovation designed by Ivanka Trump in September 2010." When I stayed at the property after the renovation, the enhancements and new look to the guest rooms was quite evident. It is yet another example of Trump the businessman maintaining and enhancing his brand.

In a February 22, 2016 press release announcing that four Trump Hotel properties were recognized with the Forbes Five-Star Award, Ivanka Trump said, "We are extremely honored to receive the prestigious Forbes Five-Star award rating," and went on to say that "Trump Hotels is one of the fastest-growing global luxury hotel companies, and it is incredibly rewarding to see our properties maintain their position year after year as the best in the world." The apple doesn't fall far from the tree.

In 2017 Forbes awarded five stars to Trump New York, Trump Chicago, and Trump Waikiki. In 2018 and 2019 the Forbes Five-Star award went to Trump International Washington DC. This is a particular feat, since it is highly unusual for a property not yet open for two years to receive the prestigious prize. AAA awarded five stars to Trump New York and Trump Chicago. AAA reviews more than 27,000 hotels with the five stars going to just 0.4% of the properties. On one of my trips to Trump Tower I was able to peek into Mr. Trump's office (he was not there). What struck me were the walls covered with framed magazine covers featuring Trump's photo, the stacks and stacks of other printed materials with positive mentions of his name and/or companies and the vast amount of memorabilia of all things Trump. Clearly, he has to have the validation and admiration of those around him, which he then proudly showcases. Again, the image of Trump as a winner.

A self-made man who is generally recognized as a winner is Howard Schultz, former Starbucks Chief Executive Officer. I lived in Seattle almost thirty years ago and had never heard of Starbucks, which is headquartered there, until then. At the time Starbucks was a much smaller company. I marveled at the fact that in winter weather, including snow, people would line up inside the Pike Place store to buy coffee. What was it about that brand that enjoyed so much success, starting with selling one simple product and then becoming an international company selling much more than coffee? For one, their leader was unconventional in his approach to business, his partnerships with the community, how he treated employees, and his corporate responsibility initiatives.

What I didn't know was that Howard Schultz grew up with two siblings in the Canarsie, Brooklyn, New York housing projects. His father, who held various menial jobs, never made more than $20,000 a year. Howard was good in sports and saw that as a way out. He was the first in his family to graduate from college, but upon graduation had no real plan for a career. Howard's dad died of lung cancer in 1988 when Howard was 36. He said that he vowed then if he ever made it big "he wouldn't leave people behind" as a legacy to his dad.[2] He went to work as a salesman for the Xerox Corporation and transitioned to a general manager of a Swedish coffee maker in 1979. While in Seattle visiting Starbucks on behalf of his employer, he became impressed with them and joined the team as Director of Marketing in 1982. At the time, Starbucks had five retail stores, an outgrowth from their Pike Place Market store which had opened in 1971. Schultz was instrumental in persuading the owners to offer espresso and other beverages which he had enjoyed in Italy. By 1986, after raising the necessary money, the first Il Giornale store opened. After two years the owners decided to focus on Peet's Coffee & Tea and sold the retail unit to Schultz and Il Giornale for $3.8 million.

Schultz re-branded Il Giornale with the Starbucks name and started his effort to expand across the country. By 1992 the company had gone public under the moniker of SBUX. During his first tenure as CEO, from 1986-2000, Schultz did many innovative things with respect to running the business. He pioneered giving part-time workers health insurance benefits and those working 20+ hours a week free tuition through Arizona State University's online programs. Schultz is also a strong advocate of community and supporting employees' volunteerism efforts.

After leaving Starbucks the first time, Schultz and ten other investors bought the Seattle Supersonics NBA basketball team and the Women's NBA Seattle Storm team for $200 million. Five years later, in 2006, he sold the team for $350 million amidst a controversy that the city of Seattle would not provide public funds to build a new arena. Schultz returned to Starbucks as CEO from 2008 to 2017. In 2010, still recovering from the 2008 recession, Starbucks was not doing very well financially. Schultz embarked on a "transformation agenda"[3] which included three prongs: community, ethical sourcing, and the environment. Starbucks committed to hiring at least 10,000 veterans and military personnel by 2018. They started the Starbucks Foundation, a nonprofit, to help strengthen the communities that they serve. Schultz figured out that putting people first and investing in them and their communities was a strong business model. He closed stores that were weak performers, hired the company's first chief information officer, and introduced the Starbucks Reward Card. By then his net worth was over $2 billion.

"Howard Schulz's story is a clear reminder that success is not achieved through individual determination alone, but through partnership and community. Howard's commitment to both have helped him build one of the world's most recognized brands."[4] Howard Schultz was passionate about playing sports, which he says gave him the opportunity to get a college education and lift himself out of poverty. He was driven to live a life and build a company with a mission to make a difference. He has authored four books, co-founded with his wife the Schultz Family Foundation supporting youth and veterans, and is now in the public arena as a possible 2020 candidate for the Presidency. Recently, Schultz, when speaking about the Democrats and his views on free enterprise said, "How many entrepreneurs in this room have been told your dream isn't going to come true?"[5] The article containing this quote goes on to say, "While building Starbucks into a successful business may not be a proxy for running the country, it was a proxy for the leadership that he would bring to the table."[6] His story truly exemplifies the American dream and the various forms that winning can take. From 2009–2017 Fortune magazine rated Starbucks as one of the world's most admired companies.

Winning on the campaign trail meant that audiences had to consist of thousands of people. In Trump's eyes his audiences were always bigger than those of any other candidate. He is a person who feeds off the energy of others; much like a comedian needs the laughter of his audience. Trump the candidate went on to bring that level of entertainment to the White House. Who else, after he signs a piece of legislation for example, turns it into a rally? He has to have the adulation – that is what keeps him going, and he reminds us of that fact over and over again. This is one of his forms of winning – receiving the applause, the chanting of "USA, USA," the wearing of the "Make America Great Again" caps. In a speech on May 20, 2016 in Louisville, Kentucky, Trump told the crowd, "We are gonna win, win, win, win. We're going to win with the military, we're going to win at the borders, we're going to win with trade, we're going to win at everything." He went on to remark that people were going to say, "Mr. President, please, we can't take it anymore, we can't win any more like this ... and I'm going to say I'm sorry, we're going to keep winning because we are going to make America great again."

Winning is part of Trump's DNA, and it was a huge part of his campaign messaging. For example, after he claimed victory in Nevada's Republican caucuses, he told a group of celebrants in Las Vegas, "And soon the country is going to start winning, winning, winning." Now, as president, he sees up close and personal how to difficult it is to win on many issues. He alone cannot fix the immigration and DACA issue, the border wall issue, or Obamacare. Winning on all of these issues will take much work, resolve, and compromise.

In the meantime, he's a man on a mission, having already announced his intention to run again in 2020. He has been raising money for the Republican National Committee and appointed a Trump Organization employee, Brad Parscale, as his co-campaign manager along with John Pence, the nephew of Vice-President Mike Pence, with Michael Glassner as executive director. Trump is consistent in the use of "Make America Great" and is a master at using that brand to sell hats, shirts, and a variety of other merchandise to raise funds for his party! I don't believe there has ever been a president who, after an election win, has so quickly begun to campaign for re-election. Interestingly, Ronald Reagan's slogan during the 1980 campaign was "Let's Make America Great Again," at a time when the U.S. economy was in deep trouble. Trump, who used different versions of the slogan prior to the 2016 presidential campaign, has said that he was not aware that Reagan used a similar phrase. He also noted that President Reagan did not trademark the slogan. In his quest to ensure the brand, candidate Trump registered the "MAGA" name, and signed an application with the U.S. Patent and Trademark Office for exclusive rights to use the phrase for political purposes. It was registered as a trademark on July 14, 2015. Millions of dollars were raised by selling "MAGA" hats at $25.00 each. Trump would frequently wear one at a rally and often pointed out those in the crowd who were also wearing one. After the election, his original campaign website transitioned to greatagain.gov. President Trump has suggested that his 2020 campaign will use the slogan "Keep America Great," and he has already asked an attorney to have it trademarked.

I believe that Mr. Trump utilized a winning approach with his campaign. In addition to perceiving the negativity and often malaise that existed in the electorate, he traveled anywhere and everywhere, went on any talk show or radio broadcast, and employed social media and the traditional written press to get his message across. Trump said that "I won the 2016 election with interviews, speeches, and social media. My use of social media is not presidential – it's MODERN DAY PRESIDENTIAL." These words, of course, refer to his use of Twitter. The home page of the donaldj.trump website currently (as of this writing) lists "News, Gallery, About, Follow Us, Shop, and Contribute. People are asked to "Help fulfill our promise to Make America Great Again!" Everything from a car bumper sticker for $4.00 to MAGA hats to T-shirts and hoodies are for sale. It's amazing how he has not only branded "Make America Great Again" but has used it consistently and effectively in his formal addresses to the American people, his rallies across the country, and in thousands of tweets.

As president he frequently talks about trade and how the U.S. is losing the trade war with China. He calls on American companies to come back to America and to manufacture their products in the U.S.A. For decades businessman Trump has had ties, trinkets, and other items made in China. Ivanka Trump produced a line of clothing, shoes, handbags and other items in China. The Trumps won in that regard, as the cost of labor is much cheaper in China. I wonder if American companies, which are frequently asked by the president to manufacture in America, are questioning why the Trumps are not putting Americans to work to produce their products. President Trump's promise in his inaugural speech was: "We will follow two simple rules: buy American and hire American." After the election, there was a huge movement to boycott Ivanka Trump's merchandise. Shannon Coulter started a #GrabYourWallet campaign in October, 2016, after the Billy Bush tape in which Mr. Trump talked about grabbing women by the p***y. She said that the tape inspired her to start the campaign. Shortly thereafter, retailers started dropping Ivanka Trump's products.

The biggest controversy came from the retailer Nordstrom, which announced on February 2, 2017, that they would no longer carry Ivanka Trump's brand, based on poor sales during the previous year. Six days later, on his personal Twitter account, Trump blamed the decision on politics, and said "My daughter Ivanka has been treated so unfairly by @Nordstrom. She is a great person – always pushing me to do the right thing! Terrible!" So, three weeks after taking office and stating that "the president can't have a conflict of interest," he was criticizing companies that no longer purchased his daughters' products! One could argue that his statement is a father standing up for his daughter, but it looked more like a president who could not distance himself from his family's brand or financial interests. Then the stakes got even higher when Kellyanne Conway, counselor to the president, commented on national television that people should buy Ivanka's products. Some say that it was a spontaneous remark and that some of what was and is going on is based on the naiveté of those who lack political experience. Kellyanne does not fall into that category. Either way, the administration believes that Nordstrom dropping the Trump brand was the result of the company disagreeing with Trump policies. After all, the decision to drop Ivanka's brand was made after Nordstrom executives said President Trump disparaged Muslims; and the Nordstrom family issued a memo to their employees about their family's ties to immigrants and how valuable they are to our country.

Most people know that the majority of clothing purchased in America is made outside of the United States. Go into any retail store and read the labels: made in China, Bangladesh,

Vietnam, Thailand. It is rare to see a "Made in the USA" label. Unfortunately, manufacturing clothing abroad is part of America's long history of companies looking to make things as inexpensively as possible, and that has resulted in production overseas and less work for Americans, but cheaper prices for consumers. Trump has said he would like to make his items in the United States, but it is hard to find companies that will do it. At the same time President Trump was touting "buy American," his daughter's company was importing 53 metric tons of Chinese goods including shoes, handbags, and clothing. Mr. Trump defended his practice of manufacturing goods overseas in 2015 when, in a CNN interview, he said that it's "not at all hypocritical to outsource because China manipulated their currency to such a point that it's impossible for our companies to compete." Regarding manufacturing Ivanka's brands in the United States, Abigail Klem, President of the Ivanka Trump brand, said, "It's great to say we want to do all of this, but we want to make responsible business decisions too ... from a business perspective, we have to have longevity."[7] Ms. Klem's comments are not unlike those of many companies that do business overseas. Since this controversy Ivanka Trump has opened a small retail store right in Trump Tower. She licenses, like her father, the Trump name to wholesale companies, and she trademarked the "IT" (Ivanka Trump) letters with the US Patent and Trademark office for jewelry, bedding, and baby products. The IT brand has also launched an e-commerce site.

Winning takes place with unlikely people from all over the world. Tony Melendez is a Nicaraguan-born foot guitarist. Tony was born without arms at a time when pregnant women with morning sickness were prescribed certain drugs which often resulted in birth defects. Tony's parents took him to

Los Angeles so he could be fitted with prosthetics, which he wore as a small child. Tony dreamt of being a singer rather playing an instrument. "It just kind of happened ... I wasn't even really looking to play the guitar. I just started messing around with it, and it just kind of worked."[8] He never took a formal lesson, yet learned to play piano, harmonica, and guitar with his feet. While in high school Tony became very involved in his church, playing up to five masses on a Sunday. People began taking notice, and he was asked to audition, at age 25, for the visit to Los Angeles of Pope John Paul II in 1987. Tony was selected to play and sing and he performed "Never Be the Same" for the Pope. He was flabbergasted when, after the song ended, the Pope himself approached Tony on stage, kissed him and said, "Tony, you are truly a courageous young man. My wish is that you continue to give hope to all the people."[9] The next year, Tony and his brother established a partnership and created "Toe Jam Music." His phone started ringing after his performance for the Pope, and it has not stopped. Since that time over 30 years ago, Tony has performed all over the United States and in 44 countries. He sang the National Anthem at the fifth game of the 1989 World Series and performed four more times for the Pope. In addition to his composing and singing, Tony is a keynote speaker as a contemporary Christian artist. In 1989, in addition to recording his first album, Tony authored his best-selling autobiography, *A Gift of Hope*. Tony is featured in *Chronicles of Courage: Very Special Artists* by Jean Kennedy Smith and George Plimpton.

Tony relocated from Los Angeles to Branson, Missouri with his wife and children. He has said that music opened the door to his dreams. Tony founded Tony Melendez Ministries, a nonprofit "dedicated to bringing compassion and hope through music and personal triumph."[10] His is a remarkable story of a small child born without arms who found a way to win – to learn, on his own, to play an instrument he loves, and to share his talent with the world in a most unlikely fashion.

Some may ask, what has President Trump "won" thus far in his presidency? On the White House.gov website, there are fact sheets for numerous categories (economy, budget, etc.) and links to articles and Trump speeches about those topics. The fact sheet is entitled "President Donald Trump 500 Days of Winning on the World Stage." Under the opioid crisis, "How We Will Win the War on Opioids." My point here is that it is no accident that articles, speeches, tweets, and interviews consistently use the word win or winning. It is a subtle and effective use of a word that President Trump savors. Journalists and writers tend to use the word often as well. In a February 25, 2018 *Politico* article, "Trump is Winning Are you Sick and Tired of it Yet?" the writer says that Donald Trump is on track to "win reelection to [the] Presidency of the United States."[11]

Some of the accomplishments of Trump's first two years include the most significant tax policy overhaul since 1986, the $1.5 trillion Tax Cuts and Jobs Act. In describing it Trump said, "Paychecks are climbing. Tax rates are going down. Businesses are investing in our great country. And, most importantly, Americans are winning." American families and businesses received $3.2 trillion in gross tax cuts and the child tax credit was doubled. Additionally, the corporate tax rate was lowered from 35 percent to 21 percent. In general, the tax cut is giving families more money and making business more competitive. Nearly 3 million jobs have been created since Trump took office, including 304,000 manufacturing and 337,000 construction jobs. Unemployment is below 4 percent, the lowest in eighteen years. The White House website includes "America is Winning on the World Stage," noting the move of the United States Embassy in Israel to Jerusalem, strikes against Syria, increased defense spending, and working with our allies to rid the world of ISIS.

In a December 14, 2017 *Huffington Post* article entitled, "Sadly, Trump is Winning" the writer says "Trump's biggest win, though, has come on three fronts. One is the GOP ... he is the point man for GOP policy and issues." She goes on to write, "The second front he's winning on is the continuing love fest that his devout base has with him." And "the third winning front for Trump is his perennial ace in the hole: the media. He remains a ratings cash cow for the networks and makes stunning copy for the print media." According to the Association of American Publishers, book sales, including audio books "are also soaring, up 20 percent in the first eight months of 2018 ... sales of political e-books rocketed by 106 percent, largely due to *Fire and Fury*.[12]

Appointing Neil Gorsuch to the Supreme Court was the first big win for the president. After Justice Kennedy announced his retirement, the president nominated Brett Kavanaugh, who came with an impeccable resume, education, and experience. Mired in a web of sexual accusations, Kavanaugh and his first accuser testified before the Senate Judiciary Committee for all the public to see. In the end, Trump's nominee was confirmed by a slim margin of 50–48.

In print media articles after President Trump had touted his accomplishments, one writer opined that "Trump's winning streak rivals one of the greatest streaks in sports" which he stated was UCLA basketball coach John Wooden's 88 straight wins over three seasons in the 1970s.[13] In a

CNN article, "The exhausting first year of Donald Trump's presidency" (January 15, 2018), Stephen Collinson says of Trump, "While he's doggedly carried out some of the most controversial campaign promises, Trump's wins have been overshadowed by behavior that electrifies his supporters but causes offense to many others."

Whether he is at Trump Tower, the White House, or particularly at Mar-a-Lago, Mr. Trump has a winning attitude. "No matter what else is happening in the world, he is treated like royalty at Mar-a-Lago."[14] He was the underdog in the campaign, yet he beat the establishment and won election to the presidency. He shocked the world in November of 2016, and there is no telling what shock waves we will feel as his first term comes to a close. With the Mueller report concluded and not accusing President Trump, his campaign, or his associates of any crime, this is perhaps the biggest win of his presidency. Trump has reiterated "My life has been about victories. I've won a lot. I win a lot. I am – when I do something, I win."[15]

Talking about winning may be the easiest discussion to have with a single person, a group of students, or a session of business leaders. People in all walks of life relate to those who they see as winners.

Again, depending on your audience, ask these questions:

- How do you define winning?

- Name someone, past or present, on a professional sports team that you view as a winner, and why do you see them that way?

- Contrast that person with someone on a team you believe is or was not a winner? Why?

- In the business world today, who do you consider a "winner"? Why?

- What adjectives would you use to describe winning?

From the start of their careers, whether in religious life or the boardroom, the successful people I speak of found ways to use the ten traits – passion, drive, enthusiasm, communicating, negotiating, loyalty, thinking big, engaging, brand, and winning. Each of them, in their own way, utilized these traits to deliver their message, start their company or organization, and build their brand.

We are fortunate to have many examples of this in every walk of life, as well as the techniques to emulate those whom we admire. There is no excuse for people who are driven to succeed not to do so. A positive attitude and daily affirmations can also help. Ridding yourself of negativity and toxic people is another way to bring more positivity into your life. Like money that begets more money, the more one is enthusiastic, positive, and hopeful, the easier the journey on the road to success.

I will admit that luck, the right relationships, and timing help. Had Donald J. Trump run for the presidency in 2012, he most certainly would not have been his party's nominee. He knew it, we knew it, everybody knew it. He waited for the right moment for his grass roots campaign (what he calls the "movement") to take hold over the Republican Party. There has never been anything like his success in American politics. The vicious campaign and subsequent election shocked the nation and the world and will be forever etched in our history. The silent majority spoke loudly on November 8, 2016. Will the 2020 election turn out the same way? As Sean Hannity often says, "buckle up". It IS going to be a bumpy ride.

More questions:

- Can someone be a winner without financial success? Describe what or who that looks like.

- What can parents do in raising their children to instill a "winning" attitude?

- What is needed to win?

- Any examples of someone who was a winner and became a loser?

- What happened?

- What does it take to keep being a "winner"?

Chapter 10 Endnotes

[1] Second Chance Act Reauthorization Act of 2018, https://csgjusticecenter.org/jc/president-trump-signs-first-step-act-into-law-reauthorizing-second-chance-act/

[2] Howard Schultz with Dori Jones, *Pour Your Heart Into It: How Starbuck's Built a Company One Cup at a Time*, (New York: Hyperion Publishers, 1997.)

[3] Kate Vandeveld, "Social Responsibility: How Starbucks is Making an Impact," www.whywhisper.co/...-responsibility-how-starbucks...

[4] Howard Schultz, *From the Ground Up: A Journey to Reimagine the Promise of America* (New York: Penguin Random House, 2019).

[5] Tanya Dua, "Former Starbucks CEO Howard Schultz warned at SXSW that Donald Trump might win again if he competes with a progressive candidate like Bernie Sanders," *Business Insider,* February 7, 2019.

[6] Ibid.

[7] Laura M. Holson and Rachel Abrams, "Tricky Stitch for Trumps: 'Made in U.S.A.' Label," *New York Times*, December 28, 2016.

[8] Brittany Gaines, "Meet Tony Melendez," *West Orange Times & Observer*, Jul. 10, 2017.

[9] Tonymelendez.com, *Toe Jam Music*

[10] Ibid., Tony Melendez Ministries

[11] Matt Latimer, "Trump is Winning Are you Sick and Tired of it Yet?" *Politico.*, February 25, 2018

[12] Claire Atkinson, "Red Hot Book Sales Show Americans Love

to read about Trump," *Association of American Publishers*, September 14, 2018.

[13] Aaron Blake, "Is Donald J. Trump the John Wooden of Presidents?" *Washington Examiner,* May 15, 2018.

[14] Laurence Leamer, *Mar-a-Lago: Inside the Gates of Power at Donald Trump's Presidential Palace* (New York: Macmillan Books, 2019).

[15] Rick Reilly, *Commander in Cheat: How Golf Explains Trump,* (New York: Hatchette Books, 2019).

Acknowledgments

Writing a book was on my bucket list ~ and with each passing birthday, the more anxious I became to complete bucket list items. I guess I will always be a doer at heart.

This book started as a dream and became a reality thanks in part to Ed Henry, chief national correspondent for Fox News. I learned that Ed was a Siena College alumnus, the same college where my oldest brother Anthony had worked decades earlier. My youngest sibling, Nicole, found Ed for me and we started corresponding. Anthony drove two hours from his home to meet Ed at what was his first book signing for *42 Faith*, at Benny's on the Beach in Lake Worth, Florida. Ed actually took the time to call me, and we engaged in an hour-long conversation about life, civility, writing, and my quest to pen a book. Ed made me realize that, as a former Trump executive, I had a story to tell, and he encouraged me to write it. I will always remember his kindness and generosity.

I have profound gratitude to my parents, who raised 11 children. My dad was fortunate in that his folks revered education so much that even through the Depression he continued his schooling and graduated from Boston Latin. Mom volunteered to drop out of school, like many, to help her family during World War II. At 14 she did piece work in a crab factory and, because of her speed, she made the most money. Dad worked two jobs for many years, and Mom was working as a waitress when she was 40 years old. My parents sacrificed much to send me and my siblings to parochial school, where I credit the Sisters for much of my learning. I read voraciously as a young girl, because reading took me all over the world while I helped care for eight younger siblings. Mom taught me the importance of writing and well into her eighties she handwrote letters, postcards, thank-yous, and birthday cards. She always remembered an occasion, a wedding, a birth, a sickness or death, including if one of our pets was sick or had passed. I am my mother's daughter.

I am also grateful to my siblings: Maria, Anthony, Roch, John, Michael, Nicole, and my cousin Tom, who were supportive, encouraging, and excited about my author adventure. They regularly asked about my progress, gave feedback, and kept me motivated. It took much more time, effort, and determination than I ever imagined, and they were with me throughout the process.

I am very fortunate to have a special man in my life who gave me the space and time I needed to accomplish my goal. Although he is legally blind, Lee painstakingly used his assistive technology to read the draft chapters of the book, offered opinions, and stayed with me each step of the way. His mother, Dorsey, was always interested in the progress of the manuscript and read one of the early drafts. And thanks to my sweet and loyal Shih Tzu, Pia, whom mom named after St. Padre Pio. She sat for hours without much attention as I labored in front of the computer in my office. She was always there to keep me company.

To my editor, Jon Harrison, who did a superb job in a timely fashion, as well as offering his honest commentary.

To Christine Keleny, publisher at CKBooks Publishing, for being responsive, informative, and helpful with the book publishing process, about which I knew nothing.

Finally, as my mom would write "PTL" (Praise the Lord), who is a source of strength to me and my family. We appreciate all of the blessings He has bestowed on each of us.

About the Author

Laurie Luongo worked in the Trump Hotel Collection as vice-president of human resources. In that role, she interacted with senior officials including Donald Jr., Ivanka and Eric Trump. She was part of the Trump team that opened five Trump hotels in three countries. She has vast experience as an executive in both the hospitality and healthcare industries. Laurie is a native Bostonian who has resided all over the United States. She is a graduate of the University of Florida and holds a lifetime certification as a Senior Professional in Human Resources. She currently works on nursing home reform while writing her second book about America's loss of civility and what must be done to get it back.

~

www.LaurieLuongo.com
@LaurieLuongo
Laurie Luongo

Made in the USA
San Bernardino, CA
01 March 2020

65001462R00124